An Ocean of the Ultimate Meaning

An Ocean
of the
Ultimate Meaning

Teachings on Mahamudra

A commentary on
Wangchuk Dorje's *Ngedön Gyamtso*

Khenchen Thrangu

TRANSLATED BY
PETER ALAN ROBERTS

Shambhala
BOSTON & LONDON
2004

Shambhala Publications, Inc.
Horticultural Hall
300 Massachusetts Avenue
Boston, Massachusetts 02115
www.shambhala.com

9   8   7   6   5   4   3   2   1

First Edition
Printed in the United States of America

⊗ This edition is printed on acid-free paper that meets the
American National Standards Institute z39.48 Standard.
Distributed in the United States by Random House, Inc.,
and in Canada by Random House of Canada Ltd

Thrangu, Rinpoche, 1933–
An ocean of the ultimate meaning: teachings on Mahamudra/
by Khenchen Thrangu; translated by Peter Alan Roberts.
p.   cm.
Includes index.
ISBN 1-59030-055-6 (alk. paper)
1. Mahāmudrā (Tantric rite)   2. Śamatha (Buddhism)
3. Vipaśyanā (Buddhism)   4. Meditation—Bka'-rgyud-pa (Sect)
5. Buddhism—China—Tibet—Doctrines.
I. Roberts, Peter Alan.   II. Title.
BQ7699.M34T47 2004
294.3'4435—dc21
2003013548

Contents

Contents

Vipashyana

Contents

Contents

Translator's Preface

The Karma Kagyu tradition, which has monasteries throughout the populated areas of Tibet, dates back to the first Karmapa, Dusum Khyenpa (1110–93), who founded three monasteries in his later years. Among these was Tsurphu near Lhasa, which was to be the seat for all future Karmapas. From that small beginning, the Karma Kagyu grew into one of the major religious traditions of Tibet. Karma Pakshi, the second Karmapa (1206–83), was the first incidence of a recognized rebirth of a lama inheriting his predecessor's authority, and this succession of Karmapa incarnations has continued to the present day. In 1475 the seventh Karmapa, Chödrak Gyamtso, established Thrangu Monastery in eastern Tibet from the ruins of a Drigung Kagyu monastery. Its first abbot, Sherab Gyaltsen, was the first Thrangu Rinpoche.

Khenchen Thrangu, the ninth Thrangu Rinpoche, whose personal name is Karma Lodrö Ringluk Marwe Sengge, was born in the region of Gawa in the east of the Tibetan plateau in 1933. At about the age of four he was recognized as the rebirth of the eighth Thrangu, Karma Tendzin Trinle Namgyal, by the twelve-year-old sixteenth Karmapa, Rigpe Dorje, and the eleventh Taisitupa, Pema Wangchuk Gyalpo.

From an early age, Thrangu Rinpoche showed great aptitude in scholarship, studying at the Thrangu monastic college under Khenpo Lodrö Rabsal from 1948 to 1953. In the late fifties, the Communist suppression of Tibetan monasteries caused him to flee to India in a large group of refugees. Surviving an intense military attack, he reached India via Bhutan in 1959. After demonstrating his scholarship by obtaining the scholastic degree of Geshe Rabjam at an examination in West Bengal—the highest degree awarded within the Gelugpa tradition of the Dalai Lama, which emphasizes scholastic studies—in 1968 Thrangu Rinpoche became the khenpo (professor) of the new Rumtek Monastery in Sikkim, India, and the tutor for the principal tulkus of the Karma Kagyu tradition.

Since the late 1970s, Thrangu Rinpoche has traveled extensively, spending most of each year teaching at centers in the Far East and the West. In 2000 the seventeenth Karmapa, Ogyen Trinley Dorje (born 1985), was recognized by the Dalai Lama and the twelfth Taisitupa in accordance with the prediction letter written by the sixteenth Karmapa, escaped from Tibet, where he was born and had undergone his early training at Tsurphu Monastery. The Karmapa currently resides in Dharamsala, India, and Thrangu Rinpoche has been appointed his official tutor.

Since 1996 Thrangu Rinpoche has taught at an annual retreat in Maine, and this book is derived from the teachings he gave there in the summers of 1998 and 1999.

The subject of this book is Mahamudra, a teaching on the practice of directly realizing the nature of the mind. The principal sources of this teaching are the meditation instructions and songs of Indian masters such as Saraha (tenth century), Tilopa (circa 928–1009), and Naropa (circa 956–1040). The greatest Mahamudra masters in the eleventh century were Maitripa and his students, in particular Vajrapani.

The Kagyu tradition itself has its source in Marpa Chökyi Lodrö (circa 1010–95), who studied under Naropa and Maitripa. This lineage, in addition to the higher tantra practices of deities such as Chakrasamvara and Vajravarahi, and the yogic practices such as *chandali,* stressed the subtle practice of Mahamudra meditation. The lineage continued to be enriched by the Mahamudra teachings of Maitripa obtained via other teachers, such as Milarepa's pupil Rechungpa (1084–1161), who studied with a pupil of Vajrapani.

The most significant transmission of Marpa's lineage came through his famous yogin pupil Milarepa (1040–1123) to Milarepa's monk pupil Gampopa (1079–1153). Gampopa, also known as Dakpo Lharje, established the first Kagyu monastery by blending the Mahamudra and Vajrayana teachings derived from Naropa and Maitripa with the scholastic, monastic, and gradualist approach of the Kadampa school founded in the eleventh century by Atisha Dipankara and his pupil Dromtön Gyalwa Jungne. A number of Kagyu traditions descend from Gampopa, collectively known as the Dakpo Kagyu, including the Karma Kagyu founded by the first Karmapa, Dusum Khyenpa.

The Mahamudra was primarily a tradition of oral instruction. Two short but significant Karma Kagyu texts on Mahamudra were written by the third Karmapa, Rangjung Dorje (1284–1339): *The Single Word Heart Teaching* (*Nying tam tsig chig*) and in particular *The Mahamudra Prayer* (*Chag chen mönlam*), which is still frequently used as the basis for Mahamudra teaching.

However, the most important Mahamudra instruction texts within the Karma Kagyu were written by the ninth Karmapa, Wangchuk Dorje (1555–1603), who presented a progressive, gradualist approach of meditation through various stages, starting with preliminary practices, going through general shamatha techniques, and passing through ever-subtler levels until the practitioner reaches the meditationless state of Mahamudra.

Karmapa Wangchuk Dorje was born in the eastern part of the Tibetan plateau. Enthroned as the Karmapa at the age of five and arriving at Tsurphu Monastery at age six, he spent most of his life in the vast mobile tent monastery of the Karmapas, traveling over the Tibetan plateau as well as to Mongolia. He composed two shorter texts on Mahamudra: *Pointing Out the Dharmakaya* (*Chöku dzub tsug*) and *Eliminating the Darkness of Ignorance* (*Marig munsel*). However, much longer is *An Ocean of the Ultimate Meaning* (*Ngedön gyamtso*).

An extensive and detailed meditation instruction text that takes an experiential and practical approach, it has been the principal manual for Mahamudra meditation in the Kagyu tradition until this time.

As Mahamudra is considered the highest teaching within the Kagyu tradition, there has been a reluctance among some lamas to make these teachings public; however, this teaching by Thrangu Rinpoche presents the entirety of the Mahamudra instructions within the Karmapa's *Ocean of the Ultimate Meaning*, with nothing hidden or held back. Moreover, they are presented in such an accessible, user-friendly way that this book may well prove easier reading than the original text itself, for Thrangu Rinpoche is well known for his ability to make the words of traditional texts become alive and applicable to people's meditation experience.

Like Karmapa Wangchuk Dorje's text, Thrangu Rinpoche's teachings are presented in three main sections: The Preliminaries; The Main Practice, divided into shamatha and vipashyana sections; and The Concluding Topics, concerning the enhancement of the practice. There is also a final section of supplementary teachings on Mahamudra. Selected terms are defined in the glossary.

This book is structured in accordance with the textual outline of *An Ocean of the Ultimate Meaning* but diverges from it in a few ways. While closely following the original text in his teachings, Thrangu Rinpoche digressed on occasion to provide explanations of the eight consciousnesses in chapter 2, the three turnings of the wheel of Dharma in chapter 6, and the philosophical arguments of the Hinayana and Mahayana schools concerning the emptiness of phenomena in chapter 9. In addition, he made only brief mention of the general and special preliminary practices, which are discussed at length in the text, and began his teaching with the four particular preliminaries of Mahamudra. With this exception, his commentary covers the complete text.

The Mahamudra eschews the elaborate, complex procedures of other more exotic methods, such as confinement in darkness, staring at the sun, and so on. It deals directly with the mind as it is without altering it in any way, raising the ordinary mind to the status of the ultimate goal. For this reason it is said that Mahamudra is hard to realize not because it is too difficult or too far away but because it is too easy and too close. The sixteenth Karmapa said that of all meditations, Mahamudra would be of the greatest benefit for Westerners, because it deals directly with the mind itself and is therefore accessible to people of any culture. Thrangu Rinpoche has consequently emphasized the teaching of Mahamudra, considering it important that this highest, or deepest, teaching should be readily available to all those who are interested in practicing it.

PETER ALAN ROBERTS, M.A. (Oxon), D.Phil.

ACKNOWLEDGMENTS

I would like to thank all those who have contributed to the creation of this book, in particular Dr. Peter Alan Roberts for his oral translation of these teachings; Bill and Jane Lawless from Vajravidya Downeast, and Steve Gilbert and Tracy Davis from Vajravidya Portland, for organizing the two summer courses in which these teachings were given; and all those who attended and assisted in these courses. I would like to thank everyone involved in the tasks of transcribing the tapes, especially Bill Lawless, and editing them into a readable book, in particular Tracy Davis as well as Emily Bower of Shambhala Publications.

Introduction

In order to develop stable and enduring love and compassion and to remove one's attachment to the self of the individual and the self of phenomena, one needs to meditate on emptiness and selflessness. There are many teachings on that meditation given in the Mahayana tradition. In the *Heart Sutra*, the Buddha taught that form is emptiness and emptiness is form. In this way, the Buddha taught emptiness and selflessness in order to benefit beings. Later, the great master Nagarjuna taught emptiness through a process of reasoning that destroys attachment to the reality of self and phenomena. Lama Mipham described this as a great reasoning process that brings certainty in unreality.

But is that certainty itself enough? No, it isn't. Even if we develop an understanding of the nature of appearances, we will need to habituate ourselves to it. In the lineage of Tilopa, Naropa, Marpa, Milarepa, and Gampopa, there are instructions that teach how to gain this realization through meditation and how to teach it to others. This is a lineage of meditation on the realization of unreality.

When the Buddha taught the *Samadhiraja Sutra*, *The Sutra on the King of Meditations*, he prophesied that his student Chandraprabhakumara, who had requested this teaching, would disseminate these teachings in the future and that the eight hundred bodhisattvas who were also present would aid him in doing so. Gampopa is said to be the rebirth of Chandraprabhakumara and to have fulfilled this prophecy.

When Gampopa received the lineage of Tilopa, Naropa, Marpa,

and Milarepa, he merged two traditions: that of the Mahayana prophesied by the Buddha and that of the meditation instructions of Tilopa, Naropa, Marpa, and Milarepa. In the union of these two traditions, meditation instructions are sometimes given in accordance with the Mahayana and sometimes with the Mantrayana. These instructions have been successively passed down through a lineage in which the instructions were given, meditated upon, realized, and then transmitted to a student.

After Milarepa had given his meditation instructions to Gampopa, Milarepa told him to go to Gampo Mountain, which was a solitary place, and practice there. Gampopa made himself a small retreat hut at Gampo Mountain and resolved to spend thirteen years there in solitary retreat. Then, in a dream, a dakini told him that thirteen years benefiting beings in that place would be better than thirteen years in retreat. Gampopa awoke and wondered how he could benefit beings, as there was no one living there. Gradually, however, the rebirths of the eight hundred bodhisattvas from the lifetime of the Buddha came to Gampo Mountain to receive his teachings, and they became eight hundred great meditators. In this way, Gampopa passed on the Mahamudra instructions.

At that time there was not one single text that taught how one proceeded from the initial stage of an ordinary being right through to the end of the path; instead, there were only short, separate instruction texts or songs on various methods of meditation and their application. The teacher would oversee the student's progress based on an oral transmission.

Eventually, Wangchuk Dorje, the ninth Karmapa (1556–1603), wrote three Mahamudra instruction texts that begin with the preliminaries to be practiced by an ordinary person and conclude with the culmination of the path. *An Ocean of the Ultimate Meaning* is the longest of Wangchuk Dorje's three Mahamudra texts.

Though there are many important teachings, I think the practice of Mahamudra is the best of all for attaining confidence and conviction. Mahamudra is a superior method that brings benefit both to this life and to future lives and is also beneficial for the ultimate attainment of buddhahood.

Studying the Dharma brings wisdom. There is the wisdom that comes from hearing the teachings, the wisdom that comes from contemplating them, and the wisdom that comes from meditation. The combination of the wisdom of meditation with the wisdom that is derived from studying the texts written by the great *siddha*s and scholars of the past will bring a very strong certainty and a clear understanding. Mahamudra meditation is beneficial for the study of the Dharma in general, as it brings stability and clarity of the mind. Therefore, Mahamudra meditation is beneficial for all situations in this life as well as for the ultimate goal.

PART ONE

THE PRELIMINARIES

I

The Particular Preliminaries

In Tibet there have been many great masters and many different Buddhist schools and teachings. Among these, the practice lineage of the Karma Kamtsang, the Karma Kagyu, is a tradition that has had a great number of practitioners with meditation experience, realization, and the accomplishment of *siddhi*s. Their accomplishment is the result of the uninterrupted transmission of the Mahamudra teachings, and we are very fortunate to be able to receive these same instructions of Mahamudra.

In the Kagyu tradition of the Vajrayana, there are two paths: the path of methods and the path of liberation. The path of methods primarily consists of the practice of the Six Yogas of Naropa. The path of liberation, the Mahamudra, can be practiced in any situation, without the need to apply ourselves to difficult techniques. The eighty-four *mahasiddha*s were able to practice Mahamudra even while performing various kinds of work, and thus they were able to attain realization. If you have all the necessary conditions to go into retreat, then you can diligently apply yourself to Mahamudra practice in that situation. But ordinary householders can also practice Mahamudra while working, as the mahasiddhas did, by keeping the mind in a relaxed state.

At the time of Wangchuk Dorje, the ninth Karmapa, there were many separate Mahamudra instructions; some were oral instructions passed on from one teacher to another, while others were written

down in various texts. Wangchuk Dorje gathered all of these together and presented them as sequential stages of meditation. His text
An Ocean of the Ultimate Meaning is divided into what are called
Dharma sections, which explain what needs to be understood, and
meditation sections, which are the actual practice instructions. Sometimes one meditation section will correspond to one Dharma section,
but sometimes one meditation section will correspond to two, three,
four, or five Dharma sections. All together there are ninety-eight
Dharma sections and about forty-five meditation sections.

An Ocean of the Ultimate Meaning is divided into three main parts:
the preliminaries, the main section, and the conclusion. The first section teaches the preliminary practices; the main section teaches the
meditation practices of *shamatha,* or tranquillity meditation, and *vipashyana,* or insight meditation; and the conclusion explains how
those who have developed experience and realization can increase
them, and how they can deal with adverse conditions and use them
to aid their practice. There is also a final section of supplementary
teachings on Mahamudra.

Although it is good to practice the meditations in the main section, it is also beneficial to practice the general and special preliminaries. Ideally, one will practice the general and special preliminaries
with diligence, as they are very beneficial for the development of the
main meditation practices. Even if one cannot do that, it is very good
to practice these preliminaries at least a little.

In addition to the general and special preliminaries, Wangchuk
Dorje teaches a third set of preliminary practices that are especially
intended for the development of Mahamudra meditation. These four
practices are called the particular preliminaries, and they are beneficial for creating stability of mind. It is taught in the Abhidharma that
there are four conditions that are necessary in order for phenomena
to occur: a causal condition, a primary condition, an objective condition, and an immediate condition. If any of these four conditions is
absent, then a phenomenon will not be perceived. Similarly, the four

particular preliminaries provide the necessary conditions for developing the realization and experience of Mahamudra meditation.

THE CAUSAL CONDITION
An Aspiration for the Dharma

The first of the four particular preliminaries is the causal condition, which is the condition that acts as a cause. The causal condition is an aspiration toward the Dharma. What prevents us from having an aspiration for the Dharma? Attachment to worldly things. We have to live in the human world, but very strong attachment prevents us from aspiring to practice the Dharma. If we think in terms of being alive for five hundred years, a thousand years, or forever, we will have a great attachment to ourselves and will not have an aspiration to practice the Dharma. Therefore, the first condition that will enable us to practice Mahamudra is to avoid thinking in that way and to lessen our attachment to this world.

This causal condition is created by meditation on impermanence, which in the beginning will develop contentment and inspire us to practice the Dharma. In the middle stage, impermanence will inspire us to continue to practice with diligence. In the end, impermanence will be the companion that has helped us to attain the final result. Even though some people have an aspiration for the Dharma, they don't actually practice it. Others practice the Dharma but don't have the diligence they need for their practice. In both cases what is missing is meditation on impermanence, which will cause one to begin and to persevere with practice.

How does one meditate on impermanence? There are many methods given in the Buddha's teachings and the commentaries, but as Milarepa said, "For me, appearances are texts." He regarded phenomena themselves as his texts, rather than trying to gain his understanding from texts that were black ink on paper. We don't need to read about impermanence in order to understand it. We can just look at appearances; at the world and how it changes; at our friends and family and the changes that happen to them. We can look at our own body, speech, and mind and understand impermanence, so that we will no longer plan what we're going to do over the next five hundred or thousand years. We can gain this understanding of impermanence simply by observing our life and its appearances. We can also gain an understanding of the impermanence of human life through the study of our culture—for example, through anthropology and archaeology.

By meditating on impermanence and gaining some understanding of it, those who are not able to enter into the Dharma will be able to enter into the Dharma, and those who have difficulty in continuing with their practice will be able to continue. In this way, we establish the causal condition. In particular, we will free ourselves of laziness, we will be able to apply ourselves, and we will progress in Mahamudra practice. Thus, the first condition, the causal condition, is developed by meditating on impermanence.

THE PRIMARY CONDITION

The Teacher

The primary condition for the development of experience and realization is devotion to and reliance on a teacher. This is because someone who has no experience of practice needs to rely on a teacher. Wangchuk Dorje describes four kinds of teachers, or spiritual friends. The first are individuals in the lineage, such as the Buddha, Tilopa, Naropa, or Marpa, who have practiced and gained realization and experience and are able to teach it to others.

We need to rely on a teacher who has experience because when we encounter difficulties in our practice, a teacher who has already encountered and overcome such difficulties can tell us what we need to do. If the favorable factors for practice are missing, we need a teacher who has experienced and overcome this circumstance and can tell us how we can gain them. Even though one teacher may not have had certain experiences, his successor will have had those experiences, and the third teacher in the succession will have had experiences that the previous teachers did not have, and so on. Thus, as Naropa said to Marpa, just as a lion cub grows up to be stronger than its mother, in the transmission of the lineage students become greater than their teachers.

A teacher who has received the transmission of the teachings can teach what qualities should be developed and how to develop them, and what faults may arise and how to eliminate them. *An Ocean of the Ultimate Meaning* describes how to develop realization and experiences, what they are, how they may diminish, and how to prevent that diminution. That is the first kind of teacher, a teacher who has received the transmission of the lineage.

The second kind of teacher is the words of the Buddha: the sutras and the tantras. By reading the commentaries on the Buddha's teaching we will learn to recognize true realization and experience and be inspired to develop them. Thus, studying the teachings of the Buddha and their commentaries is beneficial for the development of our meditation.

The third kind of teacher is appearances as signs. When in our practice we look at the true nature of phenomena, we gain certainty in impermanence, in emptiness, in wisdom, and in meditation. In this way, we develop and increase our faith and devotion, diligence, and wisdom. For example, just by observing trees, rivers, and grass, we can see that they are impermanent. This isn't realized through logical reasoning but simply by looking at what we can see. We might think the sun is eternal, but now we know that suns grow old and die, that the sun can change into a black hole. By looking at the nature of the sun, we learn to understand impermanence. Therefore, the third teacher is appearances acting as signs.

The fourth kind of teacher is the ultimate nature. This becomes our teacher when we are truly gaining results from our practice. In the Buddhist view there is a true nature to be discovered in the practice of meditation. Regardless of how things may appear, they have a true nature that can be realized. For example, we may start on the practice of shamatha in order to gain stability and calmness of mind, while not really believing that this stability of mind exists. Nevertheless, through the progressive practice of shamatha we are able to attain it. In the same way, we are seeking to attain something in vipashyana, or insight meditation. We may sometimes think that there is nothing to be gained from the practice of vipashyana meditation, but we eventually find that there is a true nature that is realized. Therefore, the fourth teacher is realization in our practice; the ultimate nature itself becomes our teacher.

Thus, we sometimes rely on a teacher who is an individual in the lineage, sometimes on the teacher that is the teachings of the Buddha, sometimes on the teacher that is the meaning of appearances as signs, and sometimes on the teacher that is the ultimate nature. It is through these four teachers that we develop our experiences and realizations.

The practice of meditation and prayer develops our devotion. We visualize that our root guru, either in his human form or as Vajradhara, is above our head, or alternatively, some people may find it easier to visualize the guru in front of them. Wherever you visualize the guru, think that this is not just imagination but that your teacher is truly present, that the wisdom and compassion of your teacher is truly present, and that by praying to your teacher you will truly receive the teacher's blessing. This is very beneficial for the development of devotion, experience, and realization.

In order to feel that you really receive this blessing of the guru, visualize that rays of white, red, and blue light come from the guru's forehead, throat, and heart. You can also imagine a ray of yellow light coming from the navel. These lights enter those same three or four places on your own body so that you receive all the blessings of the teacher's body, speech, and mind, and also a fourth aspect: the teacher's qualities. The teacher then melts into light and merges with your own body, so that your body, speech, and mind become inseparable from the teacher's body, speech, and mind.

Thus, the second condition is the primary condition: devotion to the teacher, which increases realization and experience.

THE OBJECTIVE CONDITION
Recognizing the True Nature

The third condition is the objective condition. This is the goal of our meditation. In the practice of Mahamudra one recognizes the true nature of the mind. Without thinking that this is right or that is wrong, we simply rest in meditation. But people don't recognize the true nature of the mind, and so all kinds of illusory appearances arise. We need to recognize the true nature of these illusions; otherwise, we will mistake a rope for a snake, and that mistaken perception will cause us to be afraid. In order to be free from that fear, we need to recognize that the perception of a snake is a delusion and that what we think is a snake is actually a rope.

We need a method in order to recognize this true nature. One approach is to analyze through logical reasoning. This is a stable approach, but the resulting knowledge is difficult to apply in meditation. However, through the practice of meditation we can have a true recognition of the nature of mind.

THE IMMEDIATE CONDITION
Looking at Mind as It Is

The fourth condition is the immediate condition: to look at the nature of mind exactly as it is. This does not mean, however, that you create something new in your meditation. If, while you are meditating, you think, "I'm going to have a good and pleasant experience," simply look at that thought. Or if you have an unpleasant experience, look directly at that. In this way you become free from hope and fear: the hope that meditation will go well and the fear that it will not. The very hope that meditation will go well is what stops meditation practice from progressing. Just rest in the nature of mind as it is. Thus, the immediate condition is the practice of looking directly at mind as it is, in order to be free from hope and fear.

Those are the four special conditions for the main practice of Mahamudra. You should meditate a little on each of these four preliminaries or, at the very least, seek to understand them.

PART TWO

THE MAIN PRACTICE

Shamatha

II

Essential Points of the Main Meditation

The main meditation is composed of shamatha, or tranquillity meditation, and vipashyana, or insight meditation. Happy and unhappy thoughts arise continuously in the mind. When we examine them, we see that the majority of our thoughts are unhappy. Therefore, reducing the number of thoughts is beneficial. Through the practice of shamatha we can make the mind more peaceful and stable.

We have to think, and we have lots of thoughts. We have thoughts that are unnecessary and thoughts that are necessary. When we look at our mind, we see that most of our thoughts are unnecessary, while the necessary thoughts are very few and brief. Yet from morning until night we have one thought after another, and most of those thoughts are meaningless. When we have achieved the state of shamatha, all these purposeless thoughts cease while the meaningful and purposeful thoughts become stronger and clearer, so that we know what needs to be done, we gain understanding, and so on. At present we are caught between meaningful and meaningless thoughts, and the latter are more powerful. With the development of shamatha, the meaningful thoughts increase so that we know what we have to do. We achieve understanding, wisdom, and clarity. This is called the wisdom that arises from meditation. This wisdom is not like the ultimate wisdom of a buddha; nonetheless, all unnecessary, meaningless thoughts are diminished, and the meaningful, purposeful thoughts become more powerful and clear.

ESSENTIAL POINTS OF THE BODY

Posture

We have a body and a mind. We meditate with the mind, yet the mind and body are interconnected. Machig Labdrön said that in terms of the physical posture, the body, the muscles, and all the channels should be relaxed. There are key factors of the posture of the body that are beneficial for the mind's stability. These are taught as the seven aspects of the posture of Vairochana.

The first of these seven aspects concerns one's sitting position. Sit on a cushion in a cross-legged position so the mind doesn't go to sleep. The mind needs to be stable but not dull—one needs clarity. Standing up does not provide stability, and lying down is too relaxed and produces stupor. So one sits on a cushion if one is able, or in a chair if one has problems with the legs or body.

The second point concerns the placement of the hands. The hands should be resting evenly, placed together below the navel with the palms facing up, right hand on left. This discourages the arising of thoughts. Or, alternatively, the hands may rest evenly on the knees, as taught by the third Karmapa in *The Direct Recognition of the Three Kayas*.

The upper arms should be lifted slightly upward, which creates firmness and alertness for the meditation. This is the third point.

The fourth point is that the throat should be pulled in. In the Zen tradition it is taught to pull the chin in; in the Tibetan tradition it is taught to pull the throat in. These instructions are the same. This is because if one is having a lot of thoughts, the throat extends outward.

The back should be straight as an arrow, not bent over or leaning to the side. This creates stability for the mind. If the body is straight, the channels will be straight. If the channels are straight, the airs will be straight and the mind will be calmed. This is the fifth point.

The sixth point has to do with the eyes. The eyes should look beyond the tip of the nose. Look into the space in front of you, four finger-widths in front of the nose. This basically means looking straight ahead. Don't look up like those who believe in deities, and don't look down like the *shravaka*s. In the Vajrayana, we look straight ahead with the vajra gaze. Closing the eyes might improve stability, but keeping the eyes open without distraction can bring greater clarity. This sixth point concerning the eye gaze is very important. The mind should rest with what is seen by the eyes without exploring or getting involved in what is seen, which creates thought. For example, if you see the color blue, don't think "blue." Don't be too tense, because this can bring discomfort, and don't be too relaxed, as this may cause seeing double. If you can gaze without any thoughts arising, you can achieve greater clarity.

The tongue should rest against the upper palate. This prevents the formation of saliva so that continual swallowing doesn't become a distraction. It also helps in developing stability and clarity. This is the last of the seven aspects of the posture of Vairochana.

All these points help the mind gain stability. As the *chöd* practitioner Machig Labdrön said, "We have to develop relaxation." The muscles in the limbs should not be tense. It is possible to sit in the seven-point posture of Vairochana and be tense. Relaxation of the limbs of the body is important. If one relaxes the body, the mind will be more relaxed.

There are also the five dharmas of meditation, praised by Marpa. This posture instruction is less relaxed than the seven-point posture of Vairochana.

The first of these five is called "straight like an arrow." One positions the back so that it goes beyond the point of being perfectly straight, just as when one straightens a bent arrow and has to bend it even farther in the other direction. When the central channel is bent (usually forward), it is empty. By applying a little more tension and actually bending back a little, this allows the air to enter the central channel.

The second is "throat like a hook." Again this helps the air in the central and side channels to flow properly. The hook straightens the channels and modulates the air rising in them so there are fewer thoughts and therefore greater stability.

Third, "legs interwoven." This is the vajra posture, which is like latticework and is beneficial for stability of mind.

The fourth point is "bound as in chains and fetters." The meditation belt holds the meditator in the appropriate posture.

The fifth point is "tight like vowels." Two of the Sanskrit vowels, *ri* and *li*, are a little tighter and harder to say than the Tibetan vowels. One practices in a way similar to these, and with this tight posture and controlled state, stability, warmth, and bliss can arise.

Generally, we use the seven-point posture of Vairochana. Occasionally, however, one can try this posture; it is a tighter posture that can be useful if one is experiencing dullness or stupor.

Dusum Khyenpa, the first Karmapa, said that in order to attain stability of mind we have to have the right posture. In order to see the stability of mind, we work with the stability of the body. The example he used was that in order to really see the mountain one is on, one must go over to another mountain and look back.

To help us do this meditation, we imagine the guru over our head and ask for his blessing. The guru melts into us, creating stability of mind and auspiciousness for meditation.

ESSENTIAL POINTS OF THE MIND
The Eight Consciousnesses[1]

In the sutras sometimes the Buddha taught that there are six consciousnesses and sometimes that there are eight, as two of the consciousnesses are not experienced directly.[2] First we will look at the six consciousnesses, the ones that we experience. These six consciousnesses are of two kinds: nonconceptual and conceptual.

The nonconceptual consciousnesses are the five consciousnesses that are connected with external phenomena. For example, the visual consciousness occurs through the visual faculty of the eye. Through the physical organ of the eye, there is the perception of an external object, that is, a visual form. So for a visual perception to take place, there is the primary condition—the physical organ of the eye—and there is the objective condition, the visual form, the different shapes and colors. Together, the primary condition of the organ of the eye and the objective condition of the external form give rise to the perception that occurs through the visual consciousness.

This explains how we see forms. When we hear sounds, there are the primary condition, the sensory organ of the ear, and the objective condition, the sounds. Through the presence of these primary and objective conditions, the auditory consciousness hears sounds. Next we have the primary condition of the nose as the sensory organ together with the objective condition of different kinds of smells, pleasant and unpleasant. Through that primary condition and that objective condition we have the consciousness of smell, the olfactory consciousness. The next primary condition is the tongue sensory organ. The objective condition is the different kinds of tastes, sweet, sour, and so on. Through those two conditions the consciousness of the tongue, or the gustatory consciousness, experiences tastes. These four consciousnesses are very localized. The corresponding sensory organs—eyes, ears, nose, and tongue—experience their particular sensory objects—visual forms, sounds, smells, and tastes.

It is said in the Buddhist teachings that within these physical sensory organs the actual sensory faculties exist in the form of light. For example, in the eye there is the visual faculty in the form of light, in the shape of something like the flax flower. The auditory faculty in the ear resembles a knot on a tree that is exposed when you pull the bark away. The olfactory faculty in the nose is like copper needles, and so on. The sensory faculty of the body pervades the whole body.

But none of these "forms" is visible. If you chopped off your hand or cut your arm open, you wouldn't see the sensory faculty of the body. It is beyond the scope of our visual faculties to perceive these sensory faculties. We cannot see them; they are different from other forms. Although they are included within the category of form in general, the forms of the sensory faculties are different; they are like light and cannot be seen.

Generally, when people think of the sensory faculties, they think, for example, that it is the eyes that "see." But it is not in fact the eye that sees; it is the visual consciousness within the eye that sees. In the same way, it is not the nose that smells or the ear that hears or the tongue that tastes. It is the consciousnesses within the nose, ear, and tongue that have these perceptions. These consciousnesses have the sensory faculties in the form of light as their basis. It is said that when someone dies, the light forms of the sensory faculties disappear.

While the other four sense consciousnesses are located in particular parts of the body, the consciousness of the body, the tactile consciousness, is present from the crown of the head down to the soles of the feet. The object experienced by this consciousness is everything that can be touched or felt. This tactile sensation can occur anywhere in the body—on the head, the legs, the hands, or wherever. The tactile consciousness will appear anywhere the body perceives anything that is felt or touched.

These five sensory consciousnesses—literally, the consciousnesses of the five doors—are said to be nonconceptual. The visual consciousness, for example, will see visual forms, but it does not identify these forms as being good or bad; it simply sees whatever visual forms there are without differentiating between good and bad, beautiful and ugly, and so on. And in terms of the past, the present, and the future, the visual consciousness sees only present visual forms. It doesn't see visual forms from the past or the future. Therefore, it is nonconceptual. In the same way, the auditory consciousness hears sounds, but it doesn't differentiate between good and bad sounds, and it doesn't hear sounds from the past or the future. It only hears sounds from the present. The auditory consciousness is also nonconceptual. All the five sensory consciousnesses are nonconceptual.

In addition to these five sensory consciousnesses, there is also the mental consciousness, which is the sixth consciousness. The five sensory consciousnesses perceive their objects without concepts, without any differentiation into good and bad, ugly and beautiful, and so on, but the mental consciousness does make these differentiations. It thinks, "This is good, this is bad. This has this name; this has that name. This is how this object was in the past; this is how it will be in the future." This idea of names and the ideas of past and future become mixed with the sensory perceptions. Therefore, the sixth mental consciousness is conceptual.

How does this sixth mental consciousness experience its objects? In contrast to the visual consciousness, for example, which sees forms, the mental consciousness has no direct perception of sensory objects. It does not see visual forms or hear sounds or smell smells or taste tastes or feel tactile sensations. Instead, the mental consciousness creates its own object, which has meaning. When the sensory consciousnesses have perceived their objects, the mental consciousness creates the ideas of good and bad; it gives names to things, and it creates happiness and unhappiness. The sensory consciousnesses do not have desire, or anger, or any of the other *klesha*s, the mental afflictions. But on the basis of sensory perceptions, the mental consciousness generates the idea that this perception is good or that perception is bad. It experiences sensations of happiness and unhappiness, so there is an increase in these feelings and, consequently, an increase in the mental afflictions of aversion and attachment.

Scholars have compared the five sensory consciousnesses to someone who can see but is mute: He can see everything, but he cannot say, "This is good," or "This is bad," or explain what he sees. On the other hand, the sixth consciousness, the mental consciousness, is said to be like a blind person who is very good at talking: He can give long explanations about why something is good or bad, but he can't actually see anything. The sensory consciousnesses can perceive everything, but they don't have any thoughts or concepts. The mental consciousness doesn't perceive objects, but it can identify things. The sixth consciousness also has what is called in Tibetan *rang rig*, or in Sanskrit *svasamveda*, which is self-knowing, autocognition, or self-knowledge. Because of this, we know what we have thought; we know what we have seen and heard. We don't have to ask someone else what we have perceived; we don't have to think, "I wonder what it is I have thought." Because of this self-knowledge, we know what we experience and what our perceptions and thoughts are. This self-knowledge is like someone who can both see and talk, and it creates an interrelationship between the sensory consciousnesses and the mental consciousness. We don't have to ask the visual consciousness, "What did you see?" We know what the visual consciousness is seeing. We know what the auditory consciousness has heard; we don't need to ask. And the mind also knows what "itself" has thought. The mind, therefore, knows what has occurred or what is occurring in all the consciousnesses. The sixth consciousness itself is conceptual, but the self-knowing of the sixth consciousness is non-conceptual. It is merely the experience of the sixth consciousness. Because of this we don't have to think, "This is what I am thinking." The self-knowing of the five sensory consciousnesses are also non-conceptual.

What consciousnesses do we use in meditation, such as in shamatha, vipashyana, and creation stage meditation practices? In shamatha meditation, we are making the mind calm and stable. In vipashyana meditation, we are seeing the nature of the mind. In creation stage practice, we meditate on a deity. For all these meditation practices, we use the sixth consciousness rather than any of the five sensory consciousnesses. When we visualize a deity, we don't use the visual consciousness; we use the mental consciousness. Some people think that when they visualize a deity, the visualization should be as clear as when they see things with their visual consciousness. But that is not the case, because we don't meditate with our visual consciousness. When we meditate with our mental consciousness, the image

20

we perceive is not as clear as when we see with our eyes. Instead, we have what is called a general image, which is unclear. This mental image can become clearer as our meditation becomes more stable, but it will still be a mental image that is not as clear as a visual perception. In shamatha meditation, we also use the sixth consciousness, in which many thoughts arise. The meditation serves to stabilize that consciousness and lessen those thoughts. Similarly, vipashyana meditation also employs the sixth consciousness.

These six consciousnesses are transitory; they arise and they cease. Sometimes they are there, and sometimes they are not. But there is also a teaching that there are eight consciousnesses, of which two are continuous, unlike the other six. These two do not arise and cease; they are always present. The six consciousnesses are very vivid, and therefore the Buddha sometimes taught only six consciousnesses, because the two enduring consciousnesses are very subtle and hard to perceive. Also, the eighth consciousness, the ground consciousness, in which all karmic seeds and latencies are present, could be misunderstood to be a self. Someone could be taught about the ground consciousness and then conclude, "That ground consciousness is the self," which would be a mistake. That is why in some sutras the Buddha did not teach the seventh and eighth consciousnesses.

The seventh consciousness is called the afflicted consciousness. The afflicted consciousness itself does not accumulate any karma, but it is the ever-present cause for the arising of the kleshas. The afflicted consciousness is clinging: clinging to a self and to the belief in a self; clinging to the thoughts of "I," "me," and "other"; clinging to the thought, "This is me and those are the others." This consciousness is constantly present but in a very subtle way. Sometimes we have a strong feeling of "This is me" or "This is I," but that is the sixth consciousness, not the seventh. The sixth is a transitory consciousness, but the seventh consciousness, its belief in a self, is enduring. Whatever we are doing, the afflicted consciousness is always subtly present, even without any strong development of ignorance, attachment, or aversion. There is nothing much one can do about the seventh consciousness; there is no specific remedy or meditation to get rid of it. Meditation is all about the sixth consciousness, through the development of which the seventh consciousness will naturally diminish and disappear, though not until one reaches the seventh level of a bodhisattva, at which point it is eliminated or transformed.

When you are in a deep sleep, the five sensory consciousnesses cease—the visual consciousness does not see anything, the ear does not hear anything, the nose does not smell anything, and so on—and there are also no obvious, strong thoughts of "I" or "me." Nevertheless, the seventh consciousness is still continuously present all the time. The sixth consciousness can have varied experiences—feelings of anger, attachment, happiness, unhappiness, or a neutral state. But with the seventh and eighth consciousnesses there is no such variation; those two consciousnesses are always in a completely neutral state.

The eighth consciousness is the ground consciousness. It too is said to be a continuous consciousness, unlike the sensory consciousnesses that arise and cease. It is impermanent, in that change occurs with each instant, but it does not cease and arise in the way that the sensory consciousnesses do. The ground consciousness is vast and endures for a very long time, so that the whole of a human life is contained in the ground consciousness. Our visual consciousness sees only what is in front of our face. The auditory consciousness only hears sounds made within a few hundred yards. But the ground consciousness is vast, and whether one can directly perceive them or not, there are infinite phenomena within the ground consciousness, ready to be seen or heard, and if one encounters them, one will directly perceive them.[3] All the sensory consciousnesses and the mental consciousness arise from the ground consciousness, which is vast and subtle. Although not evident, it always has the potential to manifest.

How do the eight consciousnesses relate to the practice of meditation? In shamatha, one is making the sixth consciousness more stable and calm. Although the six consciousnesses are not enduring, there is never any cessation in their continuity. They never stop arising.

This is because of the ground consciousness, which maintains the continuity of the transitory consciousnesses. So the sixth consciousness never comes to a complete cessation. Although it may cease, it continues to arise from the ground consciousness. Shamatha meditation quells strong, coarse thoughts so that the sixth consciousness becomes stable and relaxed. However, in the relaxed state of shamatha, the mind's clarity does not come to an end, since the eighth consciousness is ever-present; thus, there is an unceasing clarity. In shamatha the sixth consciousness becomes pacified within the expanse of the ground consciousness.

The eight consciousnesses are called the principal mind. A distinction is made between the principal mind and mental events. There are fifty-one types of mental events, which are grouped into different categories. Some mental events, such as sensation, are said to be ever-present. The six consciousnesses always experience some kind of sensation, whether pleasant, unpleasant, or neutral. For the afflicted consciousness and the ground consciousness, however, there are neither pleasant nor unpleasant sensations, but there is always a neutral sensation. Therefore, sensation is an ever-present mental event. Some of these mental events occur with the sensory consciousnesses, some with the mental consciousness, and some with the afflicted and ground consciousnesses.

There are another two classes of mental events: positive and negative. There is also a class of mental events that can change from positive to negative and vice versa. All these mental events are related to the mental consciousness rather than to the sensory consciousnesses or the afflicted and ground consciousnesses. For example, faith and devotion are among the positive mental events arising in the sixth consciousness. Faith and devotion arise and cease; sometimes they are there, and sometimes they are not. Negative mental events also arise, such as craving and anger. These have subdivisions, such as manifest anger and anger that one keeps within oneself over a long period of time. There is verbal anger, which is wishing to say something unpleasant to someone, and violent anger, in which one wants to cause harm.

In the practice of meditation, from among the fifty-one mental events, we employ the positive mental events of mindfulness and awareness. We maintain mindfulness and awareness throughout meditation: We do not forget the meditation, and we remain aware of what is occurring. Normally, when we are thinking, we have neither mindfulness nor awareness, and so we have no idea what we've been thinking about. We are unaware of what has been occurring in the mind. In the practice of meditation, however, we maintain mindfulness and awareness, so that we know what has been occurring. We can say, "Well, I've been having fairly good meditation today," or else, "I'm having some distraction in my meditation." Our primary practice in meditation is to maintain these two mental events of mindfulness and awareness.

In the practice of shamatha, the mental events in the sixth consciousness, such as unhappiness, regret, worry, and so on, become pacified; the mind becomes calm and reaches a state of stability without any strong thoughts. In terms of the consciousnesses, what is occurring when you achieve this result in your meditation? Does the mind come to a stop so that you become like a stone? Or is there just a kind of emptiness, an emptiness with nothing in it—no happiness, no suffering, or anything? What exactly occurs in the mind when you achieve the result of the practice? During your progress toward the result, these eight consciousnesses become transformed; faults diminish and clarity increases until the eight consciousnesses are transformed into the five wisdoms.[4]

The attainment of buddhahood is not a state of oblivion, nothingness, or nonawareness. Through the transformation of the eight consciousnesses, through the development of clarity, there is the attainment of two kinds of knowledge: the knowledge of the true nature as it is and the knowledge of all manifold relative aspects. This is what is achieved at buddhahood when the eight consciousnesses are transformed.

III

Settling the Unsettled Mind

One enters into the Dharma through hearing the teachings, contemplating them, and then meditating. Which of these three is the most important? Both hearing and contemplating are done for the purpose of practicing meditation. It is said that the Buddha taught eighty-four thousand Dharma teachings and that these teachings can all be condensed into the following three lines. The first is, "Do as many good actions as you can." The second is, "Avoid as many bad actions as you can." How does one practice the good and avoid the bad? The third line contains the answer: "Tame your mind." You need to tame your own mind, for otherwise the mind will fall under the power of thoughts and kleshas. If the mind is tamed, it will not fall under their power, and you will be able to accomplish the good and avoid the bad. How can you tame the mind? Through the practice of meditation. That is the reason that we engage in the study and practice of meditation.

The eight consciousnesses are a state of delusion, and therefore they cause the arising of illusory appearances, the kleshas, unhappiness, and so on. Nevertheless, their true nature is clarity and emptiness. Thus, the mind is in a state of delusion in terms of its temporary aspect, but ultimately, in terms of its true nature, it has the clarity of wisdom.[1] If one can see the true nature of the ground consciousness, then one will see that the mind is the source of all the positive qualities that are described in the *Uttaratantra, The Supreme Continuum*. The *Uttaratantra* describes the qualities of buddha nature, the true nature of the mind. The four qualities of the true nature of mind are perfect purity, perfect self, perfect permanence, and perfect bliss.

The nature of the mind does not in itself have any faults. If one can just rest in the true nature of the mind, then one can rest in a state of peace and bliss. As Saraha said, "I pay homage to the wish-fulfilling jewel of the mind." The mind itself is not something bad or faulty. If you can use the mind properly, you will have bliss and peace and all the qualities of the mind. For example, if you don't know how to use a wish-fulfilling jewel, you might just ignore it or throw it away into the mud. Similarly, we have the mind, which is like a wish-fulfilling jewel. If we don't know how to use it, then we'll just throw it away into unhappiness, regret, and suffering. Instead, if we realize how to use the mind, we will know how to rest in the nature of the mind with all its positive qualities, bliss, and peace.

If our mind is bound up in regret and unhappiness and we don't recognize its true nature, then we experience a state of unhappiness and see our own mind and the minds of others as faulty. If, instead, we can rest in the true nature of the mind, then we will experience bliss and the other qualities of that true nature. If we can meditate in that way both now and in the future, then we are very fortunate, because this is the perfect meditation of vipashyana, or insight. It is also shamatha meditation, because we are resting in a state of peace, in the nature of bliss and the other qualities of the mind.

Machig Labdrön taught that the essential point in the practice of shamatha is to loosen the knots in the mind. This means to make the mind free from the arising of many thoughts and to rest in a state of peace. In *An Ocean of the Ultimate Meaning*, the shamatha meditation that is taught is presented first in general terms and then in specific terms.

THE GENERAL INSTRUCTIONS
Resting the Mind

To begin, there is a classification of the three times: the past, the future, and the present. We generally have two kinds of thoughts. The first type of thought follows after what has happened in the past. We think about what we did a year ago, or a month ago, or yesterday, following a story about what happened: "I went to this place, and I did this, and this is what I thought about." Many of our thoughts are concerned with the past. So now we try not to think about the past, because the past is gone. There isn't much benefit in thinking a lot about the past because there isn't really any object for our thoughts; the object doesn't exist, as the past is gone. Therefore, first it is said that we shouldn't engage in thoughts about the past.

The second kind of thought is thoughts of the future. How do we think about the future? We go forward to meet the future. We think, "This is what I am going to do," or "This is what I am going to say." We make plans for next year or next month or tomorrow. We can make plans for the future endlessly. It can be useful to plan for the future, but when relaxing the mind in meditation, we shouldn't engage in thoughts about the future.

If we don't think about the past and we don't think about the future, then that just leaves the present. The difference between the present and the past is that the past is a very long time, so there is plenty to think about in the past. The future is also a very long time, so we can make plenty of plans in relation to the future. But if we don't think about the past or the future, then we are left with just the present, and the present is a very short time. It can be a minute or a second. While the past and the future are long, the present is so short that we don't have anything to think about if we are looking directly into the present.

The mind and its thoughts are a little bit different from each other. In essence they are the same, but they are a little different.

When one is focused on the present so that not many thoughts are arising, even though there is a ceasing of thoughts, this isn't a ceasing of mind. The mind becomes clearer. So it is said that as a result of focusing on just the present, the mind in the present becomes clear and free of thought.

When practicing meditation, one may think, "I need my mind to become stable; it must come to rest." One can be very rigid in meditation, constantly checking to see if the mind is resting by asking, "Is my mind at rest? Is my mind at rest?" The problem here is that being rigid and continually checking whether the mind is stable actually cause the arising of more and more thoughts. Thus, you should avoid being too rigid and tight. At the same time, you shouldn't be too loose, allowing yourself to follow your thoughts without any control whatsoever. You should be able to rest in meditation in a relaxed way without being too tight or too uncontrolled.

Gampopa spoke about this point using very similar words: "Do not follow after the past; do not go forward to meet the future. Instead, just rest the mind naturally in the present awareness." One doesn't think about the past or about one's plans for the future. Instead, simply rest in the present just as it is. Whatever the mind is like in the present, one just rests in that without thinking, "I'm going to accomplish stability of mind." Instead, just rest naturally in the present as it is. If the mind is left natural and uncontrived, then like water it will become clear. In Gampopa's example, if you do not disturb water, it will naturally become clear. If you meditate in that way in the present, without looking at the past or the future, although consciousness itself does not cease, thoughts will become less and less.

Great scholars have said that the mind is a very strange thing. If you go looking for the mind, you can't find it. If you look at the mind to see what it is like, you can't see it. If you try to hold the mind, you can't hold it. If you try to send it away, it won't go. If you try to keep it somewhere, it won't stay. Thus, the mind is a very strange thing. So what do we do? We don't deliberately try to create thoughts. We don't try to control the mind by bringing it to a stop.

But neither do we ignore the mind and just let it do whatever it wants. Instead, we rest in the present awareness.

It is said that it is good for the mind to be in a relaxed state. An example is given of a person who goes somewhere to live, thinking, "I'm going to stay here. I'm not going to leave." Then sometime later the king comes along and issues a command, saying, "You have to stay here and can't go anywhere else." At this point, the person starts thinking, "I've got to escape from here, I've got to get away." But soon thereafter someone else comes along and relaxes the laws, saying, "It's all right. You're free to come and go as you like." Then that person feels more relaxed and thinks, "Well, maybe I'll stay here after all." In the same way, in meditation one may think, "I am going to meditate. My mind is going to be still and stable." But trying to force the mind to be still and stable actually causes it to give rise to even more thoughts. Instead, one should stay relaxed so that the mind naturally becomes stable.

Tilopa taught six aspects of resting in meditation. The first three are not to reflect, not to think, and not to anticipate—three very similar words in Tibetan that are related to thinking. The first one, not to reflect, means not to think about what has occurred in the past. The second, not to think, means not to think about the present. And the third one, not to anticipate, means not to think about the future. So the first three aspects basically mean not to think about the past, the present, or the future. Then Tilopa said not to meditate, meaning not to try to deliberately create a state of emptiness or nothingness or to grasp at meditation as some kind of solid object. Therefore, one should not "meditate." Also, Tilopa said that one should not analyze. Not analyzing means not thinking, "This is good, this is bad, this is worse, this is better," and so on. Finally, Tilopa's sixth point concerns what one should do, which is just to rest naturally in an uncontrived manner. So without being involved with thoughts of past, present, or future, and without meditation or analysis, one simply rests in the mind naturally just as it is. Don't reflect; don't think; don't anticipate; don't meditate; don't analyze; just rest naturally.

METHODS OF MEDITATION

There are particular methods of meditation for the beginner who has not had much experience of meditation. But even for those who have done a lot of meditation and who have gained experiences and realization in their meditation, to do a little bit of the beginner's meditation is helpful in that it can increase the stability of the mind, and by increasing the mind's stability, one increases the mind's clarity. There are some who have received pointing-out instructions, a direct introduction to the nature of the mind, from a very good teacher and have then meditated on that nature, but they haven't been able to maintain the initial experience. Some are unable to develop an experience in the first place, while others are unable to develop their experience further. The reason is that they lack stability of the mind. Therefore, it is good to engage in practices that bring about this stability. Even if you have a lot of experience in meditation, doing these practices will benefit your progress.

Focusing on an Impure Object

The following practices involve focusing the mind on an impure object and on a pure object. A pure object is said to be superior to an impure object; however, it is easier at the beginning to focus the mind on an impure object. There are two kinds of impure objects: obvious or large impure objects and subtle or small impure objects. Impure objects are all the things that we normally see—all ordinary things. So when you are in a group of people, you might focus your mind on whatever is in front of you. It could be a wall or a pillar. Focus your eyes and mind on it and maintain a state of not forgetting the object upon which the mind is focused. When we say that the mind focuses on an object, this doesn't mean that we think about the object, analyze it, or ask, "Is this good or bad? Is it big or small?" Instead, the object is simply something on which the mind focuses so that it doesn't forget to look at it. This object can be anything in your field of vision.

Focusing the mind on an object is described by Saraha as being like a Brahmin making the Brahmin thread—it has to have the right degree of tension, not too tight or too loose. As previously described, if your meditation is too tight, this just causes more thoughts to arise. If your meditation is too loose, then you become inattentive and forget the object of meditation. With the right balance between being too loose and too tight, focus the mind on the object. This is how the meditation on an obvious impure object is described.

Sometimes focus your mind on a subtle or small impure object, such as a pebble or a twig. It is beneficial to focus the mind on something small. Again, the object is just something for the mind to focus on so that it doesn't become distracted. You are not trying to analyze the object or do anything else with it. Rest in a very relaxed state with the mind remaining focused on the small object, without distraction.

One should perform all activities—walking, talking, sitting, lying down, listening to Dharma teachings, and so on—without distraction. When the mind is in a relaxed and undistracted state, fewer thoughts arise. But the clarity of the mind does not cease simply because fewer thoughts are arising. The clarity of the mind continues during these activities, while the mind is resting in an undistracted and relaxed state.

There are three other methods for focusing the mind. The first of these is looking at a candle flame. One looks at a candle flame because it has clarity and is insubstantial. However, rather than looking directly at the flame, arrange the candle so that the flame is reflected in a mirror, and then focus the mind on the reflection. The image of the candle flame is used solely as something to focus on; don't analyze it or think about its color or shape or whether it's good or bad. It is there purely as a visual image for the mind to focus on. In this way, focus without distraction for the first instant of the meditation, and then the second instant, the third, the fourth, and so on to a hundred instants. In that way, the visual image of the candle flame serves as an object for the mind's focus. Do this without distraction. This meditation is called focusing on a form.

The next method is to focus on emptiness. Look at an empty space the size of a small hole or a tiny window, and focus the mind on that empty space without being distracted by anything else. When focusing on emptiness in this way, begin with a small empty space; then increase your focus to a larger space, and then progressively larger, until you are focusing on an empty space as big as the sky. Focus the mind on that empty expanse without being distracted by anything. This meditation of focusing on empty space will naturally cause the mind to become stable.

Finally, there is a more narrowly focused meditation in which one meditates on a *bindu*, a little sphere. The place in the body where all the consciousnesses come together is the point between the eyebrows. There is a triangular bone there. Here, you meditate that in that bone is a bright white sphere about the size of a pea. Focus the mind on this bindu between the eyebrows, in a tightly controlled rather than in a relaxed way.

We have used a pillar, a twig, a candle flame, an empty space, and now a bindu as the object of meditation. These are the various ways that one practices meditation by focusing the mind on an impure object. In these meditations, although the impure objects are in front of us, we do not analyze them. They are solely reference points for the meditation, something on which to focus the mind.

Focusing on a Pure Object

For the meditation focusing on pure objects, it is taught in the *Samadhiraja Sutra* that you should place a small image of the Buddha before you and focus your mind on it with faith and devotion. Even without faith and devotion, this can serve as an image on which to focus the mind. You can meditate on an actual physical image of the Buddha, or you can visualize the Buddha in the space in front of you, with a beautiful golden body and sitting with one hand in the earth-touching mudra and one in his lap in the mudra of meditation. Imagine that this beautiful golden body of the Buddha is in front of you, and meditate on it without distraction. This is the pure image on which to focus the mind.

There will occasionally be obstacles in your meditation. Many factors can be obstacles, but they can be summarized into two types: dullness and agitation. Dullness is a lack of clarity in meditation. Agitation is too much clarity in meditation. Dullness can increase to stupor, to sleepiness. If dullness occurs during this meditation, Wang-chuk Dorje gives a remedy: Focus on the upper part of the Buddha's body. Focus on the *ushnisha*, the *urna*, or simply the Buddha's whole face.[2] On the other hand, if the mind is agitated with many thoughts arising, you will not be able to rest in a stable state. In that case, focus the mind on the lower part of the Buddha's body: the navel, the feet, the cushion, or the lion throne on which the Buddha is seated. This will act as a remedy for agitation of the mind. If your meditation is free from both dullness and agitation, then just meditate on the Buddha's body as a whole or, alternatively, on the Buddha's heart, which is the essence of the Buddha's wisdom. This will help you to develop stability and clarity in your meditation.

Focusing Internally

Normally our mind is directed outward, perceiving illusory appearances. Because our mind is habituated to this, it is difficult to turn the mind inward. Therefore, in the initial meditation practices we focus on external objects, both impure and pure. Following the explanation of the meditations that focus on external objects, Wang-chuk Dorje explains a meditation that focuses inward, on a point within the body.

Imagine that in your heart is an eight-petaled lotus on which there is a deity—Guru Rinpoche, Vajravarahi, Avalokiteshvara, or any *yidam* deity; or, if you like, you can imagine your root guru in human form or as Vajradhara. It is good if you can meditate on the body of a deity or your guru in the heart center. But if you are unable to do this, or if it causes more and more thoughts to arise, imagine a bright sphere of white light instead, and focus the mind on that. Because the mind is accustomed to focusing outward, this inward focusing is difficult at first. That is why we begin this type of meditation by focusing on a point inside the body.

Focusing without an Object

So far, all these meditations—the meditation on impure and pure objects and the meditation focused internally—use an object, a reference point. The following meditation does not have a reference point. As Maitreya taught, through first having a reference point in meditation, one can develop meditation without a point of reference. All of the previous meditations on impure and pure objects and on an internal reference point lead one to the meditation without an object. In this meditation the mind rests without any object, without thinking of anything.

This may be difficult at first, so we are first taught to meditate on the elements. We gradually progress to the meditation without an object. Think of the earth element of your body in the form of a yellow cube made of light. Imagine that this yellow cube is inside a larger white sphere of water. The white sphere, in turn, is inside an even larger red pyramid of fire, and that pyramid is inside a green hemisphere of air. Meditate that the yellow cube of earth merges into the white sphere of water. Then the white sphere of water merges into the red pyramid of fire. The red pyramid of fire then merges into the green hemisphere of air, and finally, the green hemisphere merges into space. Thus, each stage is vaster and vaster until everything finally merges into space. At this point, rest in a state without any reference point.

Focusing on the Breath

We have looked at meditation with an object and without an object. Now we look at focusing the mind on the breath. The Buddha taught that we should focus the mind on the exhalation and inhalation of the breath as a remedy for too many thoughts. There are many different methods of meditation on the breath. It isn't that one method is right and another is mistaken and shouldn't be done. The *Abhidharmakosha,* for example, lists a variety of methods of meditation on the breath: counting the breath, following the breath, six methods of meditation, and so on.

An Ocean of the Ultimate Meaning contains special oral instructions that were passed on by the great masters. There are also instructions on vipashyana that are very profound and vast. You could say that shamatha is not very profound; it does, however, provide a basis for vipashyana meditation. Therefore, the great masters of the lineage have taught these methods of shamatha as a basis for vipashyana, and at this point two methods of meditation on the breath are given.

The first method is vase breathing, of which there are two kinds. One has to do with the practice of chandali, inner heat. In that practice, one uses the activities of the channels and the airs within the body. Generally speaking, vase breathing means holding the breath within one's body for a while, but in the specific context of chandali the breath is held forcefully. The other method of vase breathing is used in the practice of shamatha, and it is not forceful. Because the purpose of shamatha practice is to make the mind peaceful and stable, this kind of vase breathing doesn't involve the channels and airs or the forceful holding or expelling of the breath. The shamatha version has a gentle and peaceful manner of holding and exhaling the breath.

In the chandali practice, one begins by expelling the stale air from the body in an elaborate procedure of nine expulsions. The shamatha version is much simpler and gentler, with just three expulsions of the stale air from the body. First, gently breathe out through the nose, expelling all the air. Do this again a second time a little stronger, and a third time stronger still. Be clear that in this practice the breathing remains gentle and is not forceful. Expel the breath three times, with the hands resting on the knees in the earth-touching posture. As you breathe in, bend the fingers inward, and as you exhale, extend the fingers outward. Then as you breathe in again, draw the fingers back in, and so on. In this way, expel the air three times.

For the vase breathing itself, sit either in the posture of the seven aspects of Vairochana or that of the five dharmas of meditation, so that the body is relaxed. Breathe in, filling the abdomen. The stomach expands outward, making a form like a vase. Think that the abdomen has become empty—filled with air, but empty. Focus the mind on that. This doesn't involve any visualization; it is simply focusing the mind on the abdomen that has been filled with air. Hold the air there, not for too long or too short a time. Do this in a relaxed and comfortable way. When you begin to feel uncomfortable, gently exhale the air. Begin this vase breathing practice by doing it three or seven times. That is the first of the methods of meditation on the breath.

The second method is counting the breath. You can count either the exhalations or the inhalations—it doesn't matter. Focusing on the breath is beneficial because the breath is not a solid thing. There is breathing in, and there is breathing out—but what is being breathed in and what is being breathed out? It is something completely insubstantial. Therefore, there will naturally be less fixation and clinging to this object of meditation. Be mindful of the inhalations and exhalations and count them. Focus on the nostrils, on the sensation of the breath coming in and going out.

There are other kinds of meditation on the breath. Meditate that the in-breath fills the whole body, or meditate that the out-breath goes out into space. You can meditate that the breath is in the form of light, and so on. In this meditation of counting each breath, the breath is merely something for the mind to focus on in order to achieve stability; therefore, simply focus on the sensation of the breath coming in and going out of the nostrils. The process of breathing remains an ordinary, normal process. At first, count the breath twenty-one times. Then, as you get more familiar with the meditation, you can count up to eighty or one hundred or whatever, and in that way you will be able to meditate without forgetting to focus on the breath. You will be clearly aware of the exhalations and inhalations, and you won't make any error in counting. This meditation on the breath is beneficial.

Another meditation on the breath that is taught in the Kagyu tradition is called the three parts of gentle breathing. Normally, breathing has only two parts, the in-breath and the out-breath. In this gentle breathing with three parts, there is inhalation, there is holding the breath, and there is exhalation. This practice makes the mind stable and stops it from becoming distracted. Breathe in for however long it naturally takes, hold the breath within the body, and then exhale. These are the three parts, and each of them should take an equal amount of time. Keep the mind focused so that it does not become distracted. If you do become distracted, you will make an error in counting or will forget to hold the breath in the body. This practice of the three stages of gentle breathing—breathing in, holding the breath, and breathing out—can be used while one is working or at any time.

These practices focus the unfocused mind and still the unstilled mind. This is the purpose of all these different methods: focusing the mind on impure objects, pure objects, the candle flame, empty space, or the bindu sphere; focusing the mind without an object; focusing the mind inwardly; and focusing the mind on the breath. All these techniques are taught for the purpose of stabilizing the unstable mind.

Do we have to practice all these different methods? No, we don't. Any one of them will bring about stability. It is useful, however, to have a range of methods. For example, we could eat just bread. Eating bread fills the stomach, but we prefer to have some variety in our diet rather than eat only bread. A restaurant that has only bread on the menu will not do very good business. In the same way, if you use just one method when you meditate, it might go very well, but if you continue to use just one method, you might become a bit bored. If this happens, you can try one of the other methods and use that instead. Having a variety of different methods keeps the mind fresh and brings more power to your meditation.

STAGES OF MENTAL STABILITY

Practicing the methods for stilling the unstilled mind brings three progressive stages of mental stability. The first of these is said to be like a waterfall. Before meditating, one was not aware of one's thoughts or of how many thoughts one had. When one begins meditation, it seems as if one has more thoughts than before. If one analyzes carefully, however, one sees that it is not so. Previously one did not notice the continual arising of many thoughts, one after another. Meditation makes one aware of this, so it appears as if there are suddenly more thoughts than before. This stage of mental stability is like watching a waterfall with all the water crashing down and leaping back up, because in trying to stop the flow of thoughts, one becomes aware of how many thoughts there are in the mind.

Through maintaining mindfulness and awareness, one moves beyond the first level of stability. The second level is said to be like a great, slow-moving river. It is not that all thoughts have ceased. There are still subtle, small thoughts arising, but there is no longer a strong flow of thoughts. Therefore, like a slow river without any waves, one's meditation has no strong or powerful thoughts, and, like the continuous movement of the river, there is still a continuity of thoughts occurring in the mind. So the second level of stability is like a slow-moving river.

The third stage is the stability of a still ocean in which there are no waves. This is a state of perfect mental stability, in which one is free of all thoughts—both subtle and strong. In *An Ocean of the Ultimate Meaning*, it is said that this third stage is not like a still sea at night but like a still sea during the day. At nighttime, it is completely dark. One may reach a state of meditation in which one is free from thought but be in a state of nothingness and oblivion, like complete darkness. That kind of stability, lacking in clarity, is not the goal. In the state of complete calm and stillness, there should also be the clarity of the mind. Therefore, Wangchuk Dorje says, "It is not a sea at nighttime; it is a sea in the daytime."

Dakpo Tashi Namgyal has taught that all three stages need a clear and sharp mindfulness and awareness of what is occurring during the meditation. If these are absent, even though you are sitting in meditation, resting in stability, you will still come under the influence of thoughts, and your meditation will be profitless. In the absence of clear mindfulness and awareness, you may think that you have been practicing shamatha, but you have actually been engaged in subtle thinking without being aware of it. If there is only the appearance of shamatha without any valid shamatha practice, it will be very difficult to make progress in meditation.

One may ask, "Well, don't mindfulness and awareness necessarily involve an observer and something that is observed?" Yes, in the practice of meditation, one does "observe" with mindfulness and awareness to see whether thoughts are arising in the mind; whether the mind is resting in a state of stability or is distracted. For meditation to progress, one needs to have very firm mindfulness and a clear awareness.

Dakpo Tashi Namgyal quotes a verse from Shantideva that is addressed to all who are practicing meditation in order to gain control of their minds. What is important for those meditators? Shantideva says, "Even at the cost of your life, maintain this mindfulness and awareness," because they are so important for the development of meditation. Shantideva says that he places his hands together in supplication, requesting meditators to rely upon mindfulness and awareness because this is of such vital importance.

In terms of the stages of meditation, this instruction on how to still the unstilled mind is for beginners. Nevertheless, it is also beneficial for those who have been practicing meditation for a long time. Many people have been extremely fortunate to meet special teachers and receive from them a direct introduction to the nature of the mind, the pointing-out instructions. This direct introduction to the nature of the mind is vipashyana, but having had that introduction, one needs to maintain and develop that insight. In order to do that, one needs to have shamatha meditation as a basis. Some people can't develop insight because they haven't developed stability of mind through shamatha. Therefore, the practice of shamatha is of great benefit both for stabilizing the mind and for increasing insight meditation. Therefore, it is very important to practice shamatha meditation.

IV

Stabilizing the Settled Mind

We have looked at the ways to settle the unsettled mind. Now we come to the instructions for stabilizing the settled state so that we can remain in that state longer. We do this by eliminating dullness and agitation, which are the defects that prevent stability. Specifically, *An Ocean of the Ultimate Meaning* teaches the methods called binding above and binding below, which are used against dullness and agitation, the two main obstacles in meditation practice.

ELIMINATING DULLNESS

Binding Above

Normally, the mind is in a state of clarity, in that there are many thoughts arising. But when we make the mind peaceful and relaxed through meditation, a state of dullness naturally occurs. There is usually a loss of clarity when we enter a peaceful and stable state, and that state can increase and become stupor. If it progresses even further, it becomes drowsiness and finally sleep.

When one is in a state of dullness, subtle thoughts are still occurring. Sometimes these thoughts can take form, so that one sees all kinds of things. A meditator might think this is a meditation experience, but in fact, it's just a state of dullness, in which all kinds of shapes, colors, or forms can appear. Thus, we need to eliminate dull-ness in meditation.

How do we remedy dullness? The text first provides a visualiza-tion. Imagine a four-petaled white lotus in your heart. In the center of that white lotus is a sphere that is completely pure and totally white, bright, shiny, and perfectly round like a very small pea. Imag-ine this in your heart. Now breathe in and hold the breath for a little while. As you exhale, imagine that this white sphere rises up and exits through the Brahma aperture at the top of your head. If you look at a skull, there is what seems like a tiny aperture at the top; this is called the Brahma aperture. From this opening, imagine that the white sphere flies out and shoots up into space and then resides high up above you. Focusing your mind on this will act as a remedy against dullness.

Next the text describes a practice in which we can use the body as a remedy for dullness: With the eyes looking upward, we hold the body firmly. Here, the body should not be relaxed.

In addition, there is also an instruction for the mind: We recall the many benefits of meditation practice and how very fortunate we are to be practicing the Dharma. Thinking in this way generates joy and happiness and uplifts the mind from dullness. Thus, one's aware-ness is sharpened and intensified rather than loosened and relaxed.

These three techniques can be used to remedy or eliminate the obstacle of dullness and drowsiness. This meditation instruction is called "the meditation of the crown adornment of Great Brahma."

ELIMINATING AGITATION
Binding Below

The second obstacle to be eliminated is agitation. Thoughts of the past may arise in the mind and go around and around, so that al-though one wishes to rest in meditation, one is constantly thinking over the past. Second, thoughts of the future may also arise. One continuously thinks about all the things one is going to do, so that the mind keeps going around and around and isn't able to rest in meditation. One may experience thoughts of regret over past deeds, which prevent one from resting in meditation. And fourth, one may experience fear or worry about something bad that might happen to oneself or others. These thoughts, which may be old patterns of agitation, cause the mind to be unstable. When we are meditating, it may seem like we have two minds: One wants to rest in meditation, and the other seems powerless in the face of thoughts about the past and the future.

The first remedy for agitation described in the text is the following visualization. Imagine that in your heart there is a black four-petaled lotus facing downward. In its center is a sphere like a pea that is completely black. Unlike the white sphere, which rose up swiftly, this black sphere goes downward very slowly, like a spider coming down on its thread. You have the feeling that this black sphere is very heavy. It goes down very slowly, until it is below the ground, where it rests. This is the visualization to remedy agitation.

Next is an instruction on how to use the body to remedy agitation: With the eyes looking downward, the body should be relaxed. The posture should not be tense.

As for the mind, one should think of impermanence and the suffering of samsara in order to develop a sad state of mind. Developing sadness and disillusionment with samsara helps to remove the mind's agitation. Thus through visualization, physical posture, and the mind, one can eliminate the fault of agitation from meditation.

Sometimes we experience strong dullness or agitation in our meditation; in such instances, we apply the visualizations of the white or black lotus, and so on, to remove the obstacle. But sometimes the dullness or agitation is subtle rather than obvious or strong. In the case of subtle agitation, stabilize the mind by thinking of the sadness of samsara; in the case of subtle dullness, encourage yourself by thinking of how fortunate you are. And on other occasions, when dullness or agitation is not particularly strong, you can apply both remedies alternately—first the remedy for dullness, followed by the remedy for agitation.

CUTTING THROUGH THOUGHTS

The great Drukpa Kagyu master Pema Karpo taught a meditation instruction whereby one immediately cuts through dullness and agitation. When dullness and agitation arise, avoid attachment to them. When one does not have attachment to a thought, one can abandon it. It often happens that a thought arises and one thinks, "Oh, what a great thought; this thought is delicious, it tastes so good, it's such an important thought." Actually that thought is absolutely nothing whatsoever. So just think, "It's just a thought and an interruption to my meditation."

When a state of dullness arises, one may feel a kind of pleasantness so that the attachment makes it difficult to eliminate that obstacle. If there were no attachment, the obstacle would be easy to eliminate. But when dullness arises, it feels nice and warm, and so attachment arises. One should avoid attachment when dullness arises.

When attachment is present, it has an effect. Even if you dispel dullness, because of attachment to it the dullness will return. You can get rid of it again, but it will still come back. Attachment will keep drawing you back to the state of dullness or to thoughts of agitation. For this reason, Pema Karpo taught that we should immediately cut through whatever arises, whether it takes the form of dullness or agitation. The moment it first appears, cut through it.

There is an instruction given by the great meditation masters of the past called "beating the pig's nose." Suppose you have a fenced-in garden of flowers and vegetables, and a pig comes along, walks up to the garden fence, and starts to make his way into the garden. If at that point you come along with a stick and whack the pig on his nose, then he won't come in—he'll run away and your flowers will be safe. If, however, you don't immediately hit the pig on the nose when he first sticks his head through the fence, he'll come through it and start eating. Once he starts eating the vegetables and flowers and develops a taste for them, then it's too late for your garden. You can beat the pig on his back as much as you like, but he'll just run around and keep eating somewhere else. In the same way, you have to get rid of dullness and agitation immediately before you become attached to them, because once you are attached they become very difficult to eliminate. Dispelling the obstacles of dullness and agitation as they arise means that one is able to maintain the continuity of meditation.

Nyima Paldarbum, a lay woman who had great wisdom and diligence in meditation, once came to Milarepa and asked, "Why are you always going around saying 'PHAT'?" Milarepa answered that PHAT was a Sanskrit syllable meaning "to sever, to cut through," and that he applied this meaning to thoughts. When thoughts arise, increase, and agitate the mind, one can cut through them with the syllable PHAT. At times, although there may be no thoughts, there may be dullness and sinking of the mind. The syllable PHAT is also recited at those times to create clarity of mind. So if there are a lot of thoughts and agitation, without having to use many remedies one can stop the continuity of thoughts just by reciting PHAT. This is an easy way to stop thoughts and eliminate dullness.

NINE METHODS FOR STABILIZING THE MIND

There are nine methods taught by the buddhas for stabilizing the mind. The first of these nine methods is just called *resting*. This means resting the mind in the present without any thoughts—not following after the past or going forward to meet the future, but naturally resting the mind in the present without any thoughts. This is something one does for short periods of time.

The second stage is called *continuous resting*. When one is resting in meditation and an obstacle arises, the obstacle is eliminated so that one can continue with the meditation. As a result of eliminating obstacles, there will be a lengthening of the state of resting in meditation. If one takes the first stage of resting as a unit of time—perhaps one minute—then in the second stage one will have doubled or tripled the length of time one can rest in meditation.

The third stage is the result of being able to rest longer in meditation. When one rests in meditation for a long time, thoughts eventually arise that become obstacles. Then the third method, which is called *definite resting*, becomes necessary. One becomes aware that thoughts have arisen and understands that they are a fault. Although it is a characteristic of the mind to have thoughts, in the stage of definite resting one acknowledges that any thoughts that arise are a disturbance to meditation. With this awareness, one eliminates the thoughts and returns to resting in meditation.

The fourth method is *thoroughly resting*. Here, the qualities of peace and stability have been developed and one is resting the mind, but an obstacle disturbs that state; the obstacle is eliminated, and one reestablishes peace and stability.

When one first rests in meditation, there is a state of clarity that is comfortable and good. But it is human nature that after a while one loses interest in things, and this causes a decline in meditation. The remedy at this point is stage five, which is called *taming* because the mind is still not tamed—it loses interest in meditation. One thinks of the various benefits gained by practicing meditation and what will not happen if one doesn't practice. One thinks how continuing in meditation will develop the qualities that can eventually be of great benefit to other beings. Thinking in this way reawakens the aspiration and diligence for resting in meditation.

Sometimes there will be joy and pleasure in meditation, but sometimes one will fall under the power of various obstacles such as dullness, agitation, and the kleshas. The main problem is that one can easily develop attachment to these obstacles. However, if one can recognize them as harmful faults that cause suffering to oneself and others, attachment won't arise, and it will be easy to eliminate them. That is the sixth method, called *pacification*. This is the ability to abandon the seductive, seemingly harmless faulty thoughts that arise in meditation.

The seventh is *thoroughly pacifying*, which is analyzing in fine detail. For example, look back at the day's meditation to see what thoughts occurred. If there had been no thoughts, there would have been continuous meditation. Realizing that thoughts of craving, anger, regret, aggressiveness, and so on are of no benefit and are only obstacles to meditation, one understands that useless thoughts are hindrances to be abandoned. At the stage of thoroughly pacifying, without employing specific remedies for specific faults, one realizes that these thoughts need to be eliminated. For example, a person in meditation might have memories of going to Disneyland and think, "Ah, yes, I went around Disneyland and saw this and that." Then later on, when examining his meditation, he sees that thinking of Disneyland created an obstacle to meditation. In this same way, we identify what happened, what is an obstacle, and what needs to be eliminated.

The eighth method of stabilization is *creating one continuum*. While resting in a relaxed state in meditation, one may think, "What is happening in this meditation?" This is a subtle but unnecessary thought that one simply doesn't need. Instead, one should just relax in the state of meditation. We have seen that there is a forceful method of cutting through thoughts as soon as they appear. There is also a method called "leaving whatever arises alone," which is applied in creating one continuum. One doesn't try to change or do anything to any thought that arises; instead, one allows the thought to cease naturally by itself.

The ninth method is that as a result of all these methods, one simply rests in the state of peace and stability. This is called *resting in equanimity*.

OTHER REMEDIES FOR DULLNESS
AND AGITATION

Mindfulness and awareness are necessary so that one is aware of what one is doing in meditation. With mindfulness and awareness one is able to see whether dullness or agitation is occurring. Thus, mindfulness and awareness are like a watchman. The watchman looks to see if there is dullness or agitation within the meditation. If neither is present, then the meditation can continue. If there is dullness or agitation, mindfulness observes this happening so that remedies can be applied. At that point, one can continue with the meditation.

Sometimes our meditation goes well, and sometimes it doesn't. At times, thoughts, kleshas, and mental negativities arise so that one is unable to develop stability of mind. This indicates that one needs to meditate on impermanence. As we said earlier, it is impermanence that first inspires one to enter into the Dharma, that encourages one to continue with the Dharma, and that finally assists one in attaining the ultimate result. Contemplating impermanence may seem unpleasant, but in the long term it's beneficial, as it will arouse your diligence to continue with meditation. This in turn will enable you to attain the ultimate result. Therefore, it's very beneficial to meditate on impermanence.

One should also meditate on the four ways of turning the mind away from samsara. These are the contemplations of impermanence, the difficulty of obtaining this precious human existence, the inevitability of karma, and samsara as a source of suffering. These meditations will encourage you to continue with practice. The contemplation of a precious human existence, with its freedoms and so on, gives you the confidence to practice the Dharma. If you have the confidence to practice the Dharma, you will have diligence. By practicing with diligence, you will be able to eliminate laziness, which is the principal obstacle to developing realization and experience.

There are different kinds of laziness. The first of these is a lack of confidence. There is no reason to lack confidence. If you think that you are bad, pathetic, and unable to achieve anything in the Dharma and therefore become despondent, you won't be able to practice meditation, eliminate faults, and develop realization and experience. You will think, "I can't do that; I can't eliminate these faults; I can't practice meditation." This self-denigration acts as an obstacle. To eliminate this, it is taught that we all have buddha nature and that we have attained a precious human existence. All beings have the essence of buddhahood within them, and so all beings are equal in their ability to eliminate faults and develop qualities. With that understanding, you can eliminate any lack of confidence, enter the Dharma, practice meditation, and develop qualities. Thus, this first kind of laziness, the lack of self-confidence, needs to be eliminated.

The second kind of laziness is the laziness of bad actions. This means that one is naturally interested in engaging in negative activities. One takes pleasure in gambling, hunting, and so on, and because of that one doesn't enter the Dharma or practice meditation.

The third kind of laziness is the laziness of idleness. With idleness one is not interested in doing either bad or good activities. One isn't interested in doing any kind of activity at all. The remedy that eliminates both the laziness of bad actions and the laziness of idleness is meditation on impermanence, which will inspire one to enter the Dharma and continue with its practice. This meditation on impermanence is particularly beneficial for eliminating both laziness and dullness.

The fault of agitation means that one's mind is lost in thinking about worldly activities. There are activities that are important and need to be accomplished, but one doesn't have to think about them continually over and over. In terms of stabilizing the mind, thinking about *any* activity—whether a positive or a negative activity, even a Dharma activity—only leads to distraction. One should understand that the practice of meditation is itself a Dharma activity, and this is what is important to accomplish.

When one's meditation is unclear or one loses interest in it, this can be the result of karma. Karma—which has been accumulated because of one's tendencies to have bad thoughts and do negative actions—will cause obstacles to meditation. The repetition of bad actions creates a strong tendency that acts as an obscuration to meditation. Therefore, in the Dharma we speak of karma and obscurations. The visualization of Vajrasattva and the recitation of his hundred-syllable mantra is a remedy for karma and obscurations. The one hundred syllables are the essence of the one hundred deities that naturally reside in one's body in the airs, channels, and bindus. So if one recites the one hundred syllables, one's bad karma and obscurations will be purified, and the obstacles to meditation will be removed. The practice of Vajrasattva is one of the preliminary practices, but even if one is not practicing the preliminaries, Vajrasattva is beneficial for purifying negative karma.

When one is stabilizing the settled mind, the experiences of bliss, clarity, and nonthought can occur. There can be a pleasant experience of bliss or an experience of clarity or an experience of nonthought, in which there is a complete, even, and still state. Not only can these experiences occur but there can also be realizations. An experience is something that arises suddenly, something that has not happened before. A meditation experience is not something bad—it's good. But developing an attachment to such an experience becomes a fault in one's meditation. Realizations are like space—they never change and will always remain. But experiences are like mists—they appear and then disappear. If you develop attachment to an experience that arises in meditation, then when it disappears you will feel disappointed and will think, "I had this really good meditation, and now it's no good anymore." Although it is the nature of an experience to disappear, you will be waiting for it to return. Your meditation will become mentally fabricated rather than a genuine state of meditation. If the experience doesn't come back, you'll be disheartened and feel that your meditation has gone poorly. Therefore, whatever experiences arise in meditation, however good they are, do not develop attachment to them. Think that it doesn't matter if experiences come and go; think that it doesn't matter if they don't come at all. Just continue with the practice of meditation.

In the Vajradhara lineage prayer, Benkar Jampal Zangpo wrote, "Revulsion is the legs of meditation," "Devotion is the head of meditation," and "Nondistraction is the body of meditation." The first line, "Revulsion is the legs of meditation," means that if you have attachment to activities and feel that you have to do this and that, such constant activity will prevent your entering and continuing with the practice of Dharma. If you are free of such attachment, you can engage in and maintain the practice of Dharma and meditation. If you have legs, you can go wherever you want, but without legs you can't go anywhere. In the same way, in order to proceed in meditation, you need to have nonattachment.

The Vajradhara prayer was written by Benkar Jampal Zangpo as the result of his many years of Mahamudra meditation. For this reason, it is very meaningful that he describes devotion as the head of meditation. In Tibetan, the word "devotion" is made up of two words, *möpa* and *gupa*. They are joined together as one word: *mögu*. *Möpa* means to have an aspiration for something, that is, to think that something is very good and to be interested in doing it. *Gupa* means respect, that is, to value something as being important. Thus, one has both aspiration and respect, and together these are *mögu*, or devotion—devotion to the teacher, devotion to the Dharma, and devotion to Dharma practice. Devotion is very important for meditation. If one has devotion, one will then develop a strong conviction in the Dharma teachings. Without devotion, one won't be able to develop conviction. At the beginning, one analyzes the Dharma by asking, "Is this path going to be beneficial for me?" When one has understood the benefit of the Dharma, one will have conviction and will follow the path and attain the ultimate result. But at some point, one must generate devotion. If one is forever examining the path without ever developing conviction in it, this becomes a fault. Without conviction in the path, one will not be able to practice and will never reach the conclusion of the path. Since we need devotion in order to attain the result, it is said, "Devotion is the head of meditation."

Past masters have used this metaphor of devotion as the head of meditation because it has a definite meaning. In proportion to the body, the head looks rather small, and without considering carefully, you might think, "Well, it's the body that is important. The head is rather tiny and not really of much importance." But this isn't so. If you didn't have your head, you would have no eyes to see, no ears to hear, and no mouth with which to eat or talk. Without that small head, the body would be useless, but with the head attached to it, the body is able to do anything. In the same way, devotion may seem rather small and insignificant. You may think, "Devotion is just belief in the Dharma. There's no great result that can come from that. Meditation practice is what's going to bring the result." But in fact, devotion is very important. Without devotion we will not be able to enter the practice of the Dharma, maintain the practice of the Dharma, or attain the result of the practice of the Dharma. Without devotion we will make mistakes. We will think the same way that we did before, and our minds will be directed outwardly. We will not see the essence of the mind. If we have this small thing—devotion—we will be able to enter and complete the entire path. Therefore, although devotion seems small and insignificant, it is in fact of great importance. That is why devotion is described as the head of meditation.

From about my fifteenth to my twenty-first year, I was an academic scholar and studied texts. I had a *khenpo* as a tutor and would ask him many questions. This khenpo said, "You're asking all these questions, but you're thinking externally—your mind is thinking outwardly. You should look inward. If you look inside, then you'll see the answers." But being an academic scholar, I thought, "What's the point of looking inward? If you can't think about something and work it out, it's useless." At that time I was reading the life stories of the great siddhas Marpa and Milarepa, and I came to feel some faith and devotion, thinking, "Wow, if only Marpa were alive! What would it be like to be with Marpa?" Then I read the life stories of the Karmapas and thought, "I can't meet Marpa, but someday I can meet the Karmapa." I developed good faith and devotion. Then at one point the Karmapa sent a letter saying that on his return from a trip to China he would go to Pelpung and that it would be good to bring the lamas and tulkus there so that he could give them teachings. The day came and I went to Pelpung, thinking, "Today is a really special day, a day like no other. Today, I am actually going to come into the presence of the Karmapa. I'm going to see him and hear his voice." I really had developed good faith and devotion.

On the day I met the Karmapa, nothing special happened. But later the Karmapa was giving an empowerment of Jinasagara, Red Avalokiteshvara, and during the empowerment I suddenly thought, "Aha! So this is what is meant by looking inward. Yes, there is something to be gained by looking inward." That happened through faith and devotion. At another time I was being given an initiation of Guru Rinpoche, and I thought, "I have to be very attentive and careful in receiving this empowerment from the Karmapa." It was something very special. I had good faith and devotion, and I saw the Karmapa as a buddha. During the initiation, while receiving the word empowerment, I had the experience of being able to look inward, to look in at the nature of the mind. That happened through having good faith and devotion in the Karmapa, and so in that way my meditation developed. Then later, I lived in Sikkim. While I was living there, my meditation did not go so well because I was living with the Karmapa. Before, I saw the Karmapa as a buddha. Now I just thought, "The Karmapa helps me, he's my friend." As a result of this, my meditation got a bit worse! That is my experience.

V

Enhancing Stability in Meditation

To still the mind in terms of shamatha, first one settles the unsettled mind. Then, having gained knowledge of how to rest in the state of meditation, one stabilizes one's meditation so that it can be maintained and continued. It is subsequently necessary to enhance this stability even further so that it can develop and progress.

Both settling the unsettled mind and stabilizing that settled state pertain to actual sessions of meditation. Enhancing or increasing that stability is practiced in both the meditation sessions and the postmeditation periods.

FOCUSING ON SENSORY PERCEPTIONS

In the postmeditation phase, one should focus one-pointedly and undistractedly on whatever one sees, good or bad, with mindfulness and awareness. In this way, one knows what one is seeing. Normally we're not aware of what we're seeing, because our mind is distracted. We should maintain mindfulness and awareness so that we are able to look without distraction at whatever appears to us in daily life. If the mind is distracted, we will simply be wandering in delusion; one delusory state will follow another, and our mind will have no clarity.

If the mind is focused on visual images, we will have stability. There is also the practice of focusing the mind on sounds. Whatever sounds appear, whether pleasant or unpleasant, focus the mind on them with mindfulness and awareness, without falling into distraction.

Focus on the visual images that appear to the eyes, the sounds heard with the ears, the smells perceived by the nose, the tastes apprehended by the tongue, and whatever sensations of touch are experienced by the body. In short, all sensory perceptions are an object of focus for one's meditation. Thus, in a relaxed state of mind, focus one-pointedly with mindfulness and awareness on the five objects of perception. This is the postmeditation practice. Doing this practice will benefit your meditation during the sessions, while resting in the meditation session will also benefit your postmeditation practice. Jamgön Kongtrul addresses this point in his text *Creation and Completion*, asking, "Can one habituate oneself to a state of meditation only through periodic meditation practice?" He answers, "No, one cannot." He says that although periodic meditation practice is beneficial, one cannot habituate oneself to the state of meditation through that alone. One needs to have a continuity of mindfulness and awareness. Meditation sessions alone will not work; one needs to cultivate mindfulness in the postmeditation state. Then one will develop stability in meditation. Therefore, it is important to use the five sensory consciousnesses as a focus for one's meditation.

FOCUSING ON THOUGHTS

One can also use the sixth consciousness, the mental consciousness, as a focus for one's meditation. In the sixth consciousness many thoughts arise. Generally speaking, there are negative thoughts, which should be eliminated, and positive thoughts, which should be cultivated. There are also neutral thoughts, which are neither positive nor negative; they don't have to be either eliminated or cultivated. All three kinds of thoughts can arise in the mind. In the practice of vipashyana, one looks at the essence of these thoughts, but in shamatha practice one uses these thoughts as the focus of one's practice in order to bring about stability of mind. In the practice of shamatha, when negative thoughts arise, such as anger, jealousy, pride, craving, or ignorance, one uses them as the focus of one's meditation. Although these thoughts are kleshas, in this instance they are not to be eliminated. The idea here is to utilize whatever arises in the mind.[1] Any thought that arises becomes the object of the mind's attention, and, using mindfulness and awareness, one focuses on that thought without distraction.

Thus, when a good thought arises, such as one of generosity, good conduct, patience, love, or compassion, do not try to cultivate it, but use it purely as the reference point for mindfulness and awareness. Neutral thoughts—"I'm going to go, I'm going to sit, I'm going to eat," whatever they may be—are neither good nor bad; usually, we neither eliminate nor cultivate these thoughts. You should focus with mindfulness and awareness and without distraction on these neutral thoughts. In this way, you can use these three types of thoughts—good, bad, and neutral—as a basis for the development of stability. This instruction was given by Wangchuk Dorje on the basis of his own experience. He said that one should be aware of all thoughts that arise, but whether they are positive or negative, one shouldn't do anything about them. Instead, one should just remain in a relaxed state and observe them with mindfulness and awareness.

Some people might feel uncomfortable with this instruction. They might say that negative thoughts of ignorance, craving, pride, anger, jealousy, and so on should be eliminated and that positive thoughts should be cultivated. On the contrary, Wangchuk Dorje taught that if one sees certain thoughts as negative and to be eliminated and others as positive and to be cultivated, this will only cause more thoughts to arise and will make it very difficult to develop shamatha. Although, generally speaking, it's true that negative thoughts are thoughts that one should eliminate and positive thoughts are thoughts that one should cultivate, in this context of developing the relaxed, stable state of shamatha, one does not do that. One doesn't think of thoughts of attachment and aversion as faults, and one doesn't think of good thoughts as having good qualities. Instead, one merely remains in an utterly relaxed state, simply observing all thoughts with mindfulness and awareness and without cutting the cord of mindfulness. "Without cutting the cord" means without losing one's mindfulness and awareness. Maintain mindfulness and awareness, stay in a completely relaxed state, and just observe whatever thoughts arise, whether they're positive, negative, or neutral.

Thus, whatever thoughts arise, don't try to stop them. Just allow thoughts to flow, one after another. However, don't lose your attention; don't allow thoughts to arise without being aware of what you are thinking. Instead, maintain mindfulness and awareness and allow whatever thoughts arise to flow one after another. Mindfulness is there, however, so that not even one thought will arise without your being aware of its arising. You are aware of every single thought that arises; you are never inattentive. In this way, using mindfulness and awareness, the free flow of thoughts itself becomes the basis for shamatha and therefore the basis for the development of stability.

Look at each thought and observe whatever is there. If a thought disappears, then observe that. If a thought doesn't disappear, then observe that. If a new thought comes along, observe that with mindfulness and awareness. Observe whatever is happening; don't try to cause something to disappear. Just look at the nature of that thought. You aren't trying to alter or change the thoughts but to recognize if a thought arises and if it disappears. We are normally unaware of our thoughts. Usually our thoughts are unobserved; they come and go, and we don't know what the mind is thinking. We should always be aware of what's happening. If a thought disappears, let it disappear. If the thought doesn't disappear, that's fine, too. If a new thought wants to come, let it come. Just watch what happens with mindfulness and awareness.

If you can meditate in this way in both the meditation and

postmeditation periods, it will be very beneficial for the development of stability. During meditation you might feel that there are so many thoughts arising that the meditation is degenerating. You should take a different attitude: Just rest in meditation using whatever thoughts arise as the object or basis for the meditation. The multitude of thoughts themselves become the object of the meditation.

Thus, we have seen two ways of focusing the mind: one using the objects of sensory perception and one using thoughts. Apart from a slight difference in terms of the object of focus, these meditations are the same. One can experience visual form, sound, smell, and so on, or one can look at various thoughts of ignorance, positive thoughts, or neutral thoughts. In each case the various objects simply become the reference for resting in meditation. The great masters have taught that this is extremely beneficial for developing stability of mind. The master Yanggönpa said that in meditation one should not identify anything as a fault to be eliminated. If a thought arises, one shouldn't think, "This is something I must get rid of." Instead, whatever thoughts arise in the mind, maintain strong mindfulness and awareness so that you know what is occurring at all times.

Yanggönpa also said that in meditation one shouldn't have a de-liberate intention. One shouldn't think, "A good meditation is one in which there is a reduction of thoughts; the fewer the thoughts, the better, so that is what I must try to accomplish." Instead, simply maintain good mindfulness and awareness. That will accomplish good, genuine shamatha meditation.

TIGHTENING AND LOOSENING

For the development of stability we can describe two styles of medi-tation: tight and loose. What is meant by being tight is that both the attention of the mind and the posture of the body are very tight. As an example of this, suppose you are in the midst of a thousand peo-ple, and among them is a thief. In order to find and catch the thief, your attention must be very tightly focused. Another example is that you need to count the number of people ·in a large group in the distance. Again, to do this you need very tight and focused attention. Your eyes as well as your mind must be intently focused; if either wanders, you won't be able to count all the people. Keep your mindfulness and awareness tightly focused in the same way as in these examples. In that way, there won't be any distraction, and you will be completely attentive to what is occurring. Meditation practice with very tight mindfulness and awareness is done for very short periods.

The other style of meditation is a relaxed style. It is beneficial to practice meditation in a relaxed way for longer periods of time. In the relaxed method, you meditate without any effort. As described before, just allow thoughts to flow and remain in a very relaxed state. This does not mean, however, that you abandon meditating and just let your thoughts wander without paying any attention to them. You remain aware and completely relaxed, mindful of all the thoughts that are arising.

Meditation with a tightly focused mindfulness is done for short periods of time, whereas meditation in the relaxed state, just observing the flow of thoughts, is done for long periods. Practicing these two styles of meditation is very beneficial for the development of stability.

ELIMINATING ERRORS IN MEDITATION

Wangchuk Dorje presents a set of twelve instructions concerning how to eliminate errors in meditation. These twelve are as follows:

1. Various experiences can occur in meditation. Some people want to have only good experiences; they think, "I'm going to have a really good meditation now. I'm sure I am." They try to accomplish something, which is not really correct and can be a fault. Another type of fault can happen to those who are very learned, who

have read texts and studied meditation and know this information very well. They think, "I'm going to meditate now, and I want to have a perfect, high-quality meditation. Just any old meditation is not good enough. I'm going to see what I can accomplish in this meditation." This also is a kind of fault. What will serve to remedy these faults is to dispel the idea of wanting to accomplish something good in meditation, which causes one to fabricate or create a meditation. Instead, the meditation should be relaxed, simply observing whatever happens in the mind, good or bad. If you can remain in a relaxed state and just observe whatever arises with mindfulness, that will benefit the meditation.

2. Another kind of error in meditation is actually a misunderstanding. Sometimes people think, "Everything is fine, and whatever I think about is okay," and they pay no attention to their thoughts. They just think away as they normally do. They believe that doing this is meditation, but there is no mindfulness at all of what is occurring in the mind. The remedy for this is diligence and to meditate in a tightly focused manner in order to remedy what is really just distraction.

3. Some people may have good meditation in the beginning. They are able to settle the unsettled mind and then to make that settled mind stable. But as time passes, their meditation weakens; they no longer take care of their meditation practice. Such practitioners need diligence in order to maintain the continuity of meditation.

4. Some people have good meditation experiences in the beginning, but their meditation varies. Sometimes it goes well, and sometimes it goes badly. When their meditation is going badly, they become depressed and think, "My meditation is no good anymore. Before it was good, but now it's bad." Thinking in this way is a fault. The remedy is to realize that whatever happens in meditation, it doesn't matter. If you have good meditation, focus the mind on that. Rest in meditation on that. If the meditation doesn't go well, don't try to change the bad into good; instead, rest the mind directly on the bad meditation. The "bad meditation" itself becomes the focus

of the meditation. In fact, resting the mind on bad meditation is actually better than resting it on good meditation.

5. Some people experience unhappiness in meditation and think, "This is not good. I have to eliminate this unhappiness in order to have good meditation." But that's incorrect. If you are unhappy in meditation, just rest in a relaxed way on that unhappiness, and the unhappiness will itself become relaxed. You shouldn't attempt to eliminate a state of unhappiness.

6. Some people may get lost in thoughts while meditating but be unaware of it. While sitting in meditation, at first they think, "My meditation is going very well." But then at some point they realize, "I've become distracted," and they conclude, "I have to alter this meditation and correct it in order to get back to the undistracted state I was in before." This approach is also wrong. If the meditation is going well, rest in that state, and if distraction occurs, rest in meditation on that. You don't have to eliminate something in order to get back to where you were before. Just rest with whatever is occurring.

7. Some meditators eliminate thoughts and then think, "This is emptiness." This is incorrect. That thought itself is just another thought; it is thinking, "This is emptiness." Whatever thoughts arise, whatever continuum of thoughts occurs, simply rest your mind on them in a relaxed and mindful way. There's no need to create the thought "Meditation is emptiness" or to try to dispel thoughts.

8. Sometimes so many thoughts keep coming that one isn't able to meditate. One can't recognize the thoughts as they arise. When that occurs, it's a sign of being too loose, too relaxed, and one should tighten the focus of the meditation.

9. Sometimes one is too tight in the meditation. It's as if the body and speech are tightly bound so that one becomes uncomfortable. When discomfort occurs as a result of being too tight, relax the meditation.

10. Sometimes there can be great clarity, which takes the aspect of a form that appears very vividly, such as a person, for example. It seems as if a person has actually arrived and is truly present in front

of you. If this happens, just observe it with mindfulness and awareness, and the form will disappear. Then just rest in meditation.

11. Sometimes the mind can be very wild, like a monkey inside a house that keeps running from one window to another. The mind is scampering quickly from one consciousness to another, focusing on the visual consciousness, then the auditory consciousness, then the olfactory consciousness, and so on, focusing on various sights, sounds, or smells, and moving from one to another very rapidly. At such times, observe with mindfulness and awareness each of the mind's rapid movements. By watching this rapid activity with mindfulness, you will be able to rest in a state of meditation with enhanced clarity.

12. Sometimes the mind can be very agitated, with many thoughts arising one after another. When this occurs, it should not be seen as a fault or something that has to be eliminated. Instead, merely observe the succession of one thought after another in a relaxed state. Obstacles in meditation are eliminated by observing their flow with mindfulness and awareness, and this state of agitation is handled in the same way.

Various appearances and experiences may occur in meditation, and these twelve instructions enable you not to lose control of or try to alter the meditation. You don't have to apply all twelve of these points to your practice. Basically, whatever is happening in the meditation, whether your experiences are good or bad, you should continue to maintain the meditation. All the examples explain that it is beneficial simply to keep resting in a relaxed, mindful state.

VI

Understanding Emptiness

The Three Turnings of the Dharma Wheel

Before the Buddha's lifetime, there were great scholars in India who gave teachings that used logical analysis, and there were also practitioners of meditation who had clairvoyance and miraculous powers and taught on the basis of such experiences. However, these teachers did not teach the true nature of phenomena that the Buddha would teach. For example, they taught that through logically analyzing external phenomena it could be determined that certain phenomena were empty, while other phenomena had a basis for their appearance. They also believed in an internal self that could be proven through logical presentation.

The meditation masters also taught, on the basis of their own experience, that there must be a self. Some schools taught that the self was very small, some that it was vast, and so on. They taught that external phenomena were composed of atoms. Using logical analysis, they concluded that there was a self that existed as a material thing. Or, on the basis of meditation, they thought that there was a self that was a knowing or a consciousness. Some believed that external phenomena were created by Shiva. There were many different views concerning the nature of external and internal phenomena.

Along with these different views, there were different kinds of conduct. At that time there was great inequality among the castes.

One caste was considered able to practice while others were not; this meant that there was no hope for the lower castes to be liberated. There was also inequality between the sexes. Men were considered important and very special, whereas women were considered ordinary and of no importance. It was believed that women were unable to attain enlightenment. There were bad customs, such as the tradition of a widow being burned alive on her husband's funeral pyre, and bad conduct that was practiced. When the Buddha came, he gave very different teachings. He gave a different presentation of the nature of phenomena, which could be ascertained both through logical reasoning and through the practice of meditation. In terms of conduct, he taught the equality of all people, whatever their caste, and the equality of the sexes.

In the Dharma, the Hinayana and the Mahayana teachings present different views of the Buddha. In the Hinayana it is believed that the Buddha was born through the power of his previous karma and that in his lifetime, through diligence and practice, he attained the ultimate result of buddhahood and then taught the Dharma. The Mahayana teaches that the Buddha had already achieved buddhahood as a result of many previous lifetimes of practice and accumulation of merit. Therefore, it was an emanation who appeared in this world and who created the appearance of the attainment of buddhahood for the benefit of beings. Both of these views teach about the same Buddha, who came to Bodh Gaya and achieved buddhahood there. They teach that, having achieved that enlightened state of peace, profundity, and clarity, the Buddha thought that if he tried to explain it to others, they wouldn't understand. Therefore, he decided not to teach but to stay in the forest in solitude, meditating, and he recited a verse stating this intention. But then the deities Brahma and Indra came to the Buddha and supplicated him, saying that for so many lifetimes he had had the motivation to benefit beings, and now that he had achieved the result, it would not be right for him to remain in solitude. They requested him to teach others, and in response to that supplication, the Buddha turned the wheel of Dharma.

THE FIRST TURNING

The Selflessness of the Individual

At the beginning, the Buddha taught the selflessness of the individual. He did so because of all the different views of self mentioned before: The self was consciousness, the self was matter, the self was vast, the self was small, and so on. Before the Buddha, no one had taught that there was no self. The Buddha taught that people had to become free of the kleshas. But how? People would think, "I must get rid of my defilements," but they were unable to do so. One must look for the cause, because removing the cause will eliminate the result. The Buddha said that suffering, samsara, and the defilements all arise from a root cause, and if one can eliminate the cause, then they will all cease. That cause is the belief in a self.

In believing there is a self, we think that there is a "me" and that "I" must have happiness and avoid unhappiness, and "I" must feel anger toward those who cause me unhappiness, and so on. In this way, belief in a self becomes the source of the defilements. We are very fortunate, for if the self really did exist, we could never get rid of the defilements that arise from it. But when we try to find this self, we discover that it doesn't exist; we can't find it anywhere. When we realize selflessness, the cause is eliminated, the defilements don't arise, and there is no longer an accumulation of karma or the suffering of samsara. Therefore, in order to eliminate the cause, the belief in a self, the Buddha taught the selflessness of the individual in the first turning of the wheel of Dharma.

The Buddha had realized selflessness, and he taught it to others through the explanation of the five aggregates. When we think of the self, sometimes we think of it as the body and sometimes as the mind, so there is no definite location for what we conceive of as the self. When we think of the body as the self, we think of "my mind." When we think of "my body," we are thinking as if the mind is the self and the body is less significant. But the nature of the body and the nature of the mind are not the same. We also think of the self as being a single, solid thing, rather than as something that is made up of different parts or something that changes over time. Therefore, the Buddha taught the five aggregates, showing how the body and the mind are not a single thing but are a composite.

For example, the body is not one single entity. It is composed of the head and the arms and so forth, and it is composed of blood, flesh, and bones. If you seek a single self within the body, you will never find it. The mind is composed of eight consciousnesses, so it too is not a single, solid entity; it is composed of different consciousnesses heaped together. That is the teaching of the five aggregates, or, literally, the five heaps.

We may think that the self is something that does not alter through time, that the self as a little child changes into a young person and then into an old person. If one also believes in past and future lives, then one will think that there was a self in a previous life that has continued and is now in this present life and that the self of this present life will go on to be the self of a future life. But in fact, there is no entity that goes from one life to the next or that goes from being young to being old.

In order to explain this, the Buddha taught the twelve *ayatanas*, the twelve bases. This teaching explains the absence of a self in terms of causes. For example, for an individual visual consciousness to occur, there must be present a visual sensory faculty and a visual object. Through having a visual faculty as a cause, a visual consciousness arises as a result. In terms of the auditory consciousness, one needs the sensory faculty of the ear. With that auditory faculty as the cause, an auditory consciousness arises. All the sensory consciousnesses are dependent on a sensory faculty as a cause.

In terms of results, the Buddha taught the eighteen *dhatus*, or elements. This teaching looks at the result that arises due to the presence of, for example, a visual sensory faculty and a visual object. Those two conditions create a visual consciousness as a result. The same thing occurs with an auditory faculty and a sound: Together they create an auditory consciousness, and so on. All of these faculties and their objects create the respective consciousnesses as their results.

The teaching of the ayatanas and the dhatus thus explains that there is no continuous self as an entity; instead, in each instant, there arises a result dependent on a cause. There is a continuum that changes through time, something new created in each instant. Thus, when one changes from a child to an adult, or from a previous life to this life, there is no ongoing self; there is just the continuous arising of results dependent on causes. In that way, the Buddha taught the selflessness of the individual.

The Buddha gave 84,000 different Dharma teachings, but one can categorize all of them into the three turnings of the wheel of Dharma. In the first turning of the Dharma wheel, the Buddha taught the selflessness of the individual, and the disciples of the Hinayana who have practiced that attained the result of the shravaka *arhat*.

THE SECOND TURNING

The Selflessness of Phenomena

The second turning of the Dharma wheel was more profound than the first and was given to students who had developed greater conviction and aspiration in the Dharma. In the second turning of the Dharma wheel, the Buddha gave the teachings on emptiness. These are the teachings of the Prajñaparamita, the perfection of wisdom. In the perfection of wisdom teachings, the Buddha taught not only the selflessness of the individual but also the selflessness of all phenomena.

Because the nature of all phenomena is emptiness, the Buddha taught that the suffering of samsara was not really that harmful. In terms of conduct, he also taught the practice of the six *paramitas*, or perfections. Many sutras explain the emptiness of phenomena, especially the *Heart Sutra*, in which it is taught that there is no form, no sound, no smell, no taste, no touch, and no mental phenomena.

Although the understanding of emptiness can be gained through meditation, in the second turning of the wheel of Dharma, the Buddha mainly taught methods of logical reasoning through which one can gain certainty in the emptiness of phenomena.

Great Buddhist masters composed commentaries that present this logical reasoning. Nagarjuna and Chandrakirti composed texts explaining the five great reasonings of the Middle Way. I talk about these in my book *The Open Door to Emptiness*, which presents explanations from Lama Mipham's book *The Gateway to Wisdom*. One of these great reasonings is called the great interdependence. Nagarjuna demonstrated how nothing has its own independent existence; everything arises in dependence on something else. I like to explain this reasoning using two incense sticks.

If we have two incense sticks, one that is two inches long and one that is four inches long, everyone will agree that one is short and one is long. Nobody would say that the four-inch incense stick is the short stick and the two-inch stick is the long stick. Relatively, it seems that a short incense stick and a long incense stick actually exist. But if I replace the shorter two-inch stick with a six-inch stick, then what we previously called the long incense stick is now the short one, and this new six-inch incense stick is the long one. Everyone will agree with that. The four-inch incense stick has not undergone any change; it's still exactly the same. Previously, it was the long incense stick, and now it's become the short incense stick. And if I put an even smaller, one-inch incense stick beside the short, two-inch incense stick, the two-inch stick now becomes a long incense stick.

"Long" and "short" don't truly exist. It's purely in dependence on something else that there are such things as short or long. These are actually mental fabrications. "Long" and "short" are simply labels that one creates with one's mind in relation to the dependence of one thing upon another. Short and long, good and bad, big and small, ugly and beautiful, young and old—these don't really exist. All of these are relative ideas that exist in relation to something else. One's mind grasps the idea that something is good, bad, big, small, and so on, but that's purely in relation to something else. Therefore, the nature of phenomena is emptiness.

One can prove that phenomena exist only through interdependence, but one might ask, what about the things themselves? There may be no short and no long, which are only in relation to other things, but doesn't a thing itself exist as a solid entity? Actually, things themselves do not exist either. If we take, for example, a person's hand, some would say that there is a hand there and that it exists. But if we actually analyze a hand, we see that it does not exist.

How can we say that there is no hand? We can look at each part—this is the thumb, this is the index finger, this is the ring finger, this is the external skin, there is the internal flesh, and so on. What we actually have is an aggregation of different parts. To this aggregation of different things the mind assigns the name "hand." But that's merely a name assigned by the mind, and there is no such thing as a hand.

Therefore, you might think that I exist except for my right hand! But you can analyze the left hand in the same way, so then I don't have a left hand either. The same goes for my right leg, my left leg, my head, and so on. So although it may look like there is a man sitting here, it's completely untrue—there's nobody here at all! In that way, the second turning of the Dharma wheel shows how all form is emptiness.

THE THIRD TURNING

Buddha Nature

The teachings of the third turning of the Dharma wheel clarify emptiness. It is incorrect to think that emptiness means nothing whatsoever, that is, some state in which there are neither faults nor good qualities, a mere absence of anything. That is not the case, because we perceive things. We have perception, and there is knowledge and wisdom. This is said to be the buddha nature, the essence of buddhahood. Thus, the third and final turning of the wheel of Dharma teaches that while everything is empty, there is the buddha nature.

One can gain certainty about these teachings through logical reasoning, but what is really needed is direct understanding through meditation, through the practice of vipashyana, or insight meditation. The Buddha gave this teaching of vipashyana. In addition, he taught the Vajrayana. The Vajrayana is the path of the swift attainment of realization and includes the visualization of deities, and so on. This swift path of the Vajrayana was taught, practiced, and accomplished by many great masters in India. Having gained the results of this practice, they passed on the lineage of transmission through which these teachings came to Tibet, where they became widespread. Many people received these teachings, practiced them, and gained the final result. This is not just a story—there truly are many people who attained the final result of buddhahood through utilizing this path.

Vipashyana

VII

Ascertaining the Mind's Nature

In the sutras it is taught that one must first gain an understanding of the emptiness of phenomena through logical reasoning. But to achieve buddhahood using this approach takes—as it did for the Buddha—three incalculable eons of accumulating merit. By contrast, in the Vajrayana teaching, one can attain the state of Vajradhara, the ultimate realization, in one lifetime within the same body. One might wonder how three eons' worth of accumulation of merit can be achieved in one lifetime within one body. The reason is that the sutra path and the tantra path are very different.

In the sutras, one first gains a definite understanding of the emptiness of the nature of phenomena; afterward, through meditation one gradually develops that understanding, which slowly becomes clearer and clearer. In the Vajrayana, one gains a direct experience not of the emptiness of outer phenomena but of the nature of the mind, which is swifter and easier to accomplish. The Vajrayana teaches the methods for a direct recognition of the nature of one's own mind, and by seeing the true nature of the mind, one understands the true nature of all phenomena. The realization presented here is in terms of the Vajrayana.

The path of gaining certainty through logical analysis is more easily accomplished by applying it to external phenomena, whereas a direct recognition is easier to attain by focusing on the nature of one's own mind. Therefore, we have the path of the sutras, which is the path of analysis and logical examination that brings about certainty of the nature of external phenomena; and we have the path of the Vajrayana, which sometimes also uses logical analysis but which mainly teaches the method of the direct realization of the nature of the mind. The sutra path is the path of inference. The tantra path, the Vajrayana, is the path of direct experience.

In the Vajrayana, to begin with, one develops the stability of shamatha meditation, a state of stability that has clarity, not dullness. The ninth Karmapa, Wangchuk Dorje, has described states of stability by using three examples. The first is an example of stillness and stability that has clarity. This is like a sun free of clouds. Yet sometimes it happens that thoughts arise in the mind, so in the second example, these thoughts are compared to waves on water. There is no difference between the waves and the water—they are the same. Finally, there is clarity without any attachment or grasping. This is like a baby seeing a shrine room. The baby will see all the things in the shrine room—the colors, shapes, paintings, and so on—but will have no thoughts about these things. There is simply seeing, without any ideas or concepts about what is being looked at. This is like the experience of clarity without grasping.

All the appearances that one perceives are appearances of the mind. By having the direct experience of seeing the nature of the mind, one also experiences the emptiness of all appearances. Thus, one gains the realization that one needs to gain and is able to eliminate everything that should be eliminated.

The emptiness of external phenomena is not that important, because external phenomena do not cause us great benefit or harm. More important are the mind and its nature. The great siddhas of the past taught that the body and speech that perform activities are like servants. The mind, which is the motivation, is like a king. It is one's motivation that creates what is good and what is bad. It is the mind that is of great importance.

Phenomena are appearances of the mind, and if one has a strong belief in their reality, there will be attachment, which will result in obstacles and suffering. All the various kinds of suffering that occur are the result of the mind being in a state of delusion. If one is able to see the true nature of the mind, suffering will diminish and disappear.

When one sees the nature of the mind, one sees that it is empty, but it is not simply emptiness alone. There is also the clarity of a knower: There is both knowing the emptiness of phenomena and the clarity of this knowing. These two, clarity and emptiness, are conjoined. There is emptiness while there is clarity, and that clarity has emptiness. Thus, there is omniscient knowledge: There is knowledge of the nature of phenomena (that is, seeing that the nature of all phenomena is emptiness), and there is the knowledge of the multiplicity of phenomena (knowing all the various things that can be perceived). In that way, one has a clarity that is free from attachment. This is the realization of the union of clarity and emptiness. This is the realization of vipashyana, of insight.

Vipashyana is said to be of three kinds. First, there is the insight that comes when the mind is resting at peace in a state of stability. Next, there is the insight of how the mind is while in movement. And finally, there is the insight that arises in relation to phenomena, which is the insight of the nature of perceived appearances.

There are different methods of vipashyana instruction. Some teachers give vipashyana instruction as a pointing-out instruction, or as a direct introduction. People can gain different sensations as a result of this direct introduction, which is given as some kind of sign. It is very good to have these different kinds of sensations. For some people, however, even though they have an experience, that experience then vanishes, so it actually proves to be unhelpful. Others may retain the experience but are unable to develop it. In *An Ocean of the Ultimate Meaning*, the pointing-out instruction is not based on a sensation, but rather on examining the nature of the mind through successive stages. Here the direct introduction is of three kinds: viewing the mind in stillness, viewing the mind in movement, and viewing appearances. One looks at the nature of the mind, and because this is done through successive methods of looking, a stable experience is created. Because one has gained this recognition oneself, it will not fade away. Consequently, the experience can increase and develop further through practicing the methods of enhancement. Thus, the teaching given in *An Ocean of the Ultimate Meaning* is very fruitful and beneficial.

LOOKING AT THE MIND AT REST

The state of shamatha is a state of stability with few thoughts. When we are resting in this state and the mind is at rest, we can observe it. We see that the mind is at rest with few thoughts, in a state of stillness. At this point, we look at this mind that is in stillness. We examine it, not by means of analysis or reasoning, but just by looking directly at the mind in the state of rest. There is stability and rest, but how is this happening? Who is at rest? What is it that is at rest? Where is this resting taking place? What is the nature of this resting? We look directly, not analyzing but just looking to see. Who is resting? What exactly is it that is resting? That which is resting, does it have a shape? Does it have color? Does it have location? Is it a thing? Or is it nothing? We can look directly because this is our own mind, and we are able to look directly at it to see what is there. We look to see that which is at rest.

This procedure is done through looking, through experience. One isn't saying to oneself that it *seems* as if the mind is like this or like that; this will not bring real success in meditation. Instead, one is looking, directly looking, in order to gain a direct experience of a color or a shape—is there one?—and looking to see what is there. Is there a thing, or is there nothing? If there is something, where does it arise, and where is it located? If it ceases, how does it cease? When does it cease? Where does it cease? Meditate to gain a direct experience of this. If you meditate like this and feel that you aren't able to see anything or find anything, you shouldn't become disheartened and think, "Well, I'm not able to meditate, I'm not able to see or realize anything." Instead, continue to apply yourself to the meditation with diligence.

When we look at the mind at rest in a state of stability, it is primarily the sixth consciousness that does this looking. All the other consciousnesses are also present, but we don't make a distinction between them. There's a "seer," a "hearer," a "thinker," and there is "that which is at rest." We look to see where this resting occurs. To begin with, where does it come from? Where is it? Where does it go? How and from where did it originate? How does it stop? In this way, we look to see what it is that is at rest.

When we look directly in this way, sometimes there is a state of stability, but sometimes many thoughts may arise. Sometimes strong, vivid thoughts occur, or sometimes the mind may be in a state of dullness. In those situations, we look to see what it is that's thinking the thoughts. What is giving rise to these thoughts? What is it that is in a state of dullness? We look to see the nature of what we are observing. What is thinking? What is in this state of dullness? What is in this state of calm stability? We can't identify it by location or shape, and we cannot find any real nature in that which is resting. We remain in the state of that view, the view that there is stillness, but a stillness that has no nature that can be found.

We look but are unable to find any reality to that which is at rest. Sometimes when this occurs, some people feel scared, but there is no reason to be frightened, for that is how the mind is—how it has always been, how it is now, and how it will always be. Since this is how it has always been, there is no reason to start being afraid now. And when we cannot find anything, when we fail to identify anything, that not-finding actually results in a state of peace and happiness. For example, suppose you are dreaming that you're having a nice, pleasant drive in your car, and then suddenly the car crashes and you feel very frightened. But then you wake up, happy and relieved, saying, "It was just a dream! Nothing has happened to me. I wasn't in a car crash, and I'm fine." The recognition of the nature of mind is like that: We can be sad and suffering, but when we look at the nature of the mind and can't find anything, there is relief and happiness. We realize that although there is this suffering and sadness, there isn't anything there that can really harm us. We see that there is no reality that can be found or grasped, and so we experience peace and happiness.

Having rested in the state of stability and stillness and looked at the nature of mind, the student is then questioned by the teacher. While looking at the nature of mind, has the student been able to see anything or not? Has there been some experience or not? The student may say, "I haven't been able to see anything," or "I had an experience of this or that." Some may say that there is a knower that is present. Some may say that there is a knower, but it knows nothing; there is a state of darkness, a knowing without perceiving. Someone else may say that it's a state of clarity, that there is a knower and a state of clarity that can know anything. Wangchuk Dorje provides questions that the teacher should ask the student. In working with these instructions yourself, you can examine yourself to see what has been gained from the meditation, what has been perceived or experienced.

If the experience of meditation is one of darkness or unknowing, one should apply oneself to meditation again and cultivate the meditation further. If one experiences a state of clarity in meditation, that is a good result. It means that a good experience came from the meditation. Another way of looking at the mind is as follows: One can compare this meditation of looking at the mind in stillness with one's previous practice of shamatha to see if there is a difference between them. In one's practice of shamatha, one experienced clarity and a blissful state; compared to this present meditation, however, the previous shamatha meditation did not have sufficient clarity—a clarity that is able to see the absence of anything that can be identified. So there is a difference between the shamatha meditation, in which there was a state of stability, and the present meditation on the mind resting in stability, in which there is clarity.

There is also the experience of seeing a state of peaceful resting, which has no location. There isn't anyone who is at rest; there isn't anything at rest; there is no identifiable process of this resting taking place. There is a state of being at rest, and we can look at it in terms of assessing its clarity. Is there a state of clarity, or a state of dullness? For example, a stone has no clarity whatsoever; it is in a state of nothingness. When we look at the nature of the resting state, we can look to see whether nothingness is all there is. Although there is no identifiable "rester," is there clarity?

The word *clarity* can itself be a cause of error, because sometimes people misunderstand its meaning and think that we are talking about brightness, some kind of luminosity, like moonlight, sunlight, or electric light. Clarity means that the mind knows, that it is not in a state of oblivion. There is knowledge and knowing. We know that there is a state of peace, but it is unidentifiable. Although we cannot locate it, we can see that there is also a state of clarity, a knowing.

Generally, one first establishes shamatha meditation, in which the mind does not become involved in the arising of thoughts. Shamatha achieves a state of stability. In vipashyana meditation, one looks to see what is resting in that state of stability. Shamatha meditation is just concerned with the stable state itself, while vipashyana meditation looks to identify that which is in the state of stability. And in looking, one does not find anything that has true reality. Yet there is a state of clarity or knowing that one has had from birth to the present, and it is unceasing. It is this state of clarity that will increase until one reaches omniscience, until one has the Buddha's wisdom, which sees things as they truly are and sees the various manifold things as they appear. It is this unceasing clarity that develops into omniscience.

Some people might think that this clarity is like a self, like a real entity. It isn't. When one looks, one can find no identifiable reality there. There is nothing that has any solid existence. And even though there is an absence of anything having any true or real existence, at the same time this absence of any true existence is also a state of clarity, a clarity devoid of any real existence. This is direct recognition within the state of stability.

Sometimes in practicing shamatha and vipashyana it can seem to us that there really isn't much difference between the two. It can be difficult to discriminate between them. But the state of shamatha is something that is able to overcome but not eliminate the defilements. One can't gain a special experience in the state of shamatha meditation. That insight is what is gained through the practice of vipashyana, of looking at the mind in stillness.

LOOKING AT THE MIND IN MOVEMENT

While you are resting in a state of stability, a thought arises, or you can cause a thought to arise. It may be the thought of a friend, a relative, or an enemy. Induce a thought of attachment or aversion, and then look at the mind that is giving rise to that thought. A great variety of thoughts can arise from the mind, so look at the mind that is giving rise to these thoughts. Look for a shape or a color or something that is giving rise to these thoughts. Where has this thought come from? How has this thought arisen? Who is having this thought? When you look at these thoughts, they seem nonexistent. A thought arises, but you can find no real essence to it. For example, think of New York and the Statue of Liberty. The Statue of Liberty will appear very clearly in your mind, standing there with one arm upraised, and you think, "Well, this thought is really happening, but where is it coming from? Where is it? How does it arise? Does it really exist or not?" It definitely appears to the mind, but you can't find anything that is truly existent in the thought that has arisen.

When the eyes see forms, the mind experiences those forms. Look to see what exactly is seeing these visual forms. The ears hear sounds. What is it that experiences sounds? And the same for smell, taste, and touch—look to see what is being aware of these perceptions.

On examination, you will find neither a location where the thought appears nor something that gives rise to it; it is as if the thought is not occurring. But although it is unfindable, it is still vividly happening. A thought happens, but when we examine it, we find nothing. This is what is taught in the *Heart Sutra*, which states, "Form is emptiness and emptiness is form." The thought of the Statue of Liberty occurs, but when you examine that thought, you can't find anything; there is no location, no real event that is happening. Therefore, form is emptiness. But although it is emptiness, it nevertheless also appears; while not truly occurring, it still happens. Therefore, emptiness also is form. Thus, "Form is emptiness and emptiness also is form." In this way, we can know the nature of all phenomena. This knowledge does not come from examining external phenomena but by looking at what occurs within the mind. By directly observing the mind, we can realize what the Buddha taught. This is what the Buddha meant when he said that the nature of all phenomena is the same as what one sees in one's own mind, where things seem to occur but have no true reality.

Thus, in this second way of looking at the mind, one looks at the mind in movement, the mind producing thoughts. Look at the arising of thoughts: What gives rise to these thoughts? Where do they go? Do they go to the head, the feet, the hands, the internal organs? Look to see where the mind is: Where does it reside? Where does it go? Where does the mind go in relation to the external elements and the six classes of beings? For example, if you go into a house, where does the mind go? How does the mind go into a house, and how does the house appear? When you look in this way, you will not find anything located anywhere. You will not find anything going anywhere. This not-finding is seeing the empty nature. This does not mean merely thinking about an empty nature; it means having a direct experience, a direct insight into the absence of any reality. This emptiness is not just emptiness alone, for it also has the clarity that is knowing the arising of appearances and knowing their empty nature.

Through logic one can gain an inferential understanding of

emptiness. This can be done with external forms like incense sticks, and one can also apply a similar logic to establish the emptiness of the body. But in Mahamudra meditation, the approach is not inferential but direct: One looks directly at the nature of one's own mind. In that way, one gains a direct experience of emptiness.

VIII

Cutting through the Root

Looking at the nature of the mind has two aspects. The first entails looking at the mind in stillness and the mind in movement. In addition, there is also what is called "cutting through the root." This means not merely looking at the mind but seeing that the mind is devoid of any real nature. That is, it is naturally devoid of any reality.

You seek something within the mind that is still and something within the mind that moves, and through that seeking you see that there is nothing whatsoever to be found. Look at what it is that is seeing this and try to find what sees; you will not find anything that is seeing. Then search to see what is searching, and you will discover that while there appears to be something to be looked for and something that is looking, you cannot find either of them, because their nature is emptiness. Cutting through the root means seeing the emptiness of the nature of the mind.

In this meditation, just look for the mind that is in a state of rest, and you will not be able to find anything. Do this repeatedly, over and over. Next, look to see what is looking. There is the object that is being looked for, and there is the looker. Look to see who is looking, what it is that is searching, and you cannot find anything. You are cutting through the root by looking to see the searcher, the looker: Where does it come from, where does it reside, and where does it go?

When the mind is looking at the mind, a certain doubt can arise.

In Shantideva's *Bodhicharyavatara* (*Entering the Way of Life of the Bodhisattva*) and also in Chandrakirti's *Madhyamakavatara* (*Entering the Middle Way*), it is written that the mind cannot see the mind. If we read this, we might think there is a mistake, because the Mahamudra teachings teach that the mind should look at the mind. Yet Shantideva's and Chandrakirti's texts state very clearly that the mind cannot see the nature of the mind. They even give examples. A very strong man, no matter how strong he is, cannot carry himself on his own shoulders. A very sharp knife, even though it can cut anything else, cannot cut itself. In the same way, the mind, however clear it may be, cannot see itself. The mind has clarity. It can see many different objects and different phenomena, but it cannot see itself. It cannot see its own nature. Therefore, you might think, "Chandrakirti and Shantideva say that the mind cannot see itself, and yet the Mahamudra teachings say that the mind must look at itself and see its own nature." The teachings in the wisdom chapter of Shantideva's book and the Mahamudra teachings appear to be in conflict, but in fact they are not. In the wisdom chapter of Shantideva's *Entering the Way of Life of the Bodhisattva* and in Chandrakirti's *Entering the Middle Way*, when it says that the mind cannot see the mind, it means that the mind *as an entity* cannot see the mind *as an entity*. What Shantideva and Chandrakirti are refuting is the view of the Chittamatra school, the Mind Only school, which says that the mind has a true existence and can see itself.[1]

In the Middle Way teachings of Nagarjuna, it is said that there is emptiness, but this emptiness is not nothingness. And in addition to Nagarjuna's teaching, there is also the teaching of Maitreyanatha. Their explanations are different. When Nagarjuna wrote that the nature of the mind is emptiness, he said that it doesn't exist, it doesn't not exist, it doesn't both exist and not exist, and it's not neither existent nor nonexistent. It is free from all these extremes. Emptiness is not just a simple nothingness like space. Therefore, there is also the aspect of clarity present in being beyond the extremes.

On the other hand, Maitreyanatha taught that the mind is empty but that this emptiness is not mere nothingness because there is buddha nature, the essence of buddhahood, the source of all buddha wisdom. This buddha nature exists. Thus, there is an aspect of unceasing clarity. In looking at the nature of the mind, we gain a direct recognition of this clarity. This accords with the explanations given by both Nagarjuna and Maitreyanatha.

The Mahamudra teachings do not say that the mind is an existent entity. They say that the mind has no true existence. The mind is the union of clarity and emptiness without any true existence. When the mind sees itself, sees its own nature, it sees the absence of any real nature, the absence of any true existence. It does not see itself as having a real existence. It does not look and see an existent entity. This accords with the views of Chandrakirti and Shantideva when they say that the mind is not a real thing. The mind as a real thing could not see itself. Therefore, what Shantideva taught in the wisdom chapter of *Entering the Way of Life of the Bodhisattva* and what Chandrakirti taught in *Entering the Middle Way* do not contradict what is taught in the instructions on Mahamudra about the mind seeing itself.

The teachings of great masters such as Dharmakirti and Dignaga on *pramana* (logic and epistemology) speak about a direct knowledge through self-knowing. This is in the context of relative phenomena. Therefore, when we hear the Mahamudra teaching of self-knowing, we may think it also is in terms of relative phenomena and is of no great significance. But the self-knowing in logic and epistemology is different from that in Mahamudra, where self-knowing is the mind knowing its own true nature.

In the pramana teachings, "self-knowing" simply means that the mind is not concealed from itself. This means that the mind knows what it is thinking and knows what it perceives. For example, when the visual consciousness perceives a form, the visual consciousness knows what it is seeing. When a sound is heard, the auditory consciousness knows what sound it is hearing. Whatever arises as an object of the sixth consciousness, the sixth consciousness knows what it is perceiving. In that way, the mind is not concealed from itself. What another person is thinking or seeing is concealed from us, but we know what we ourselves are thinking, seeing, hearing, and so on. That is the meaning of self-knowing in terms of relative phenomena, the way things appear.

This is different from the self-knowing of the Mahamudra. When the Mahamudra teachings use the term "self-knowing" (rang rig), it means that the mind can see the indivisible clarity and emptiness that is its nature. The mind can see its own nature. This is what is meant by self-knowing in the Mahamudra.

When we look at the nature of the mind, it is not that something new occurs. It is simply that the mind has always been directed outward and has never looked inward at its own nature. That nature has always been there, but we have not had direct recognition of it. When we look into the nature of the mind, we see its clarity and emptiness. Before we do that, it seems that the mind is something very vivid and powerful and has a solid existence. When we look inward at the nature of the mind, we can't find it. This is not because we lack the ability or don't know how to find it. The nature of the mind has always been a state of emptiness and clarity. It has never had any solid, real nature. It's not that the mind is hard to see because it is far away or very deep or vast. We can look and see the nature of the mind.

When we see the mind's lack of real existence, we understand what is meant when the Buddha taught, "no eye, no ear, no nose, no tongue, no body, no mind. . . ." We have looked and seen that there is no real existence. People might think, "What on earth can this mean? 'No eye, no ear, no nose'—it's like someone saying they don't have a head! It doesn't make any sense." But when you look and see the nature of mind, you see that this is how it is. For example, a visual consciousness has a perception of a visual object when a visual faculty, a visual consciousness, and a visual object are present. But when you look to see what it is that is seeing, you can't find anything. You can't really find this visual consciousness. It is the same for hearing sounds. Even though there is the sound, the sensory faculty for hearing sound, and the auditory consciousness, you can't find anything that is hearing the sounds.

It is the same for all the sensory consciousnesses—visual, auditory, olfactory, gustatory, and tactile—as well as the mental consciousness, which thinks. Things arise in the mental consciousness, but when you try to see what it is that is perceiving, you can't find anything. So there is no visual consciousness, no auditory consciousness, no mental consciousness, and so on, and therefore we say there is no eye, no ear, no nose, and so on, and no mind. This is not a new or changed situation. This is simply the nature of the mind.

ELEVEN ACTIVITIES OF VIPASHYANA

In describing shamatha meditation, the sutra tradition and the Abhidharma speak of nine levels of resting the mind. In the case of vipashyana meditation, these traditions list eleven mental events. Similarly, these Mahamudra instructions include eleven mental activities of vipashyana. Here we have a union of the Mahamudra instruction on vipashyana with the description of the levels of vipashyana found in the sutra and Abhidharma tradition.

The first of these eleven activities is *thorough searching*. This is a thorough inquiry, which in Mahamudra means looking at the mind. One looks at the mind to see if it is a thing or not a thing. If it's a thing, then what is its color, shape, form, and so on? If the mind is not a thing, or if it is nothing, then what is the nature of this nonexistence? In that way, one makes a thorough inquiry into the nature of the mind, not by using reasoning or analysis but by directly looking at the mind.

The second activity is called *discriminating examination*. Discriminating examination and thorough searching are more or less the same, but a slight distinction is made between them. With thorough searching, one looks to see what the mind is—is it a thing or not, and so on. In discriminating examination, one is looking for particular details. One persists in looking. One doesn't just think, "There is no color or shape," and then forget about it. Instead, one asks, "If it doesn't have a color, yet we are still saying there is a nature of the mind, then what is this nature of the mind that is without color? What is this absence of color?" If one looks for the shape of the nature of the mind and finds no shape, then one looks at the nature of the mind and asks, "What is this nature of the mind that has no shape?"

Also, when thoughts arise in the mind, stay in the mind, and then go from the mind, one looks at them. Where does the thought first arise? Where is the thought when it is in the mind? Where is the thought when it goes from the mind? In that way, one undertakes a discriminating examination.

If, for example, strong anger has arisen, where did that anger come from? Where did it arise? One could say that anger comes from thinking of an enemy or hearing harsh speech, but here the question is the *original* source of the anger. For example, if you think of a flower, where does it grow from? It grows from a certain place. One looks for a similar source of anger. One tries to find where anger is—inside the body, outside the body, or in between. If an angry thought or a pleasant thought has arisen, it is in the mind. Where in the mind is it? One tries to find that place. Finally, those thoughts vanish. Where does a thought go when it vanishes? One tries to find that location. In doing this examination, one will not find anything. One will not find a place where thoughts arise, a place where they are located, or a place where they go. The Buddha called this examination and the understanding derived from it "the three doors to liberation."

If we cannot find a place where thoughts originate, this means that there is no cause for an existent entity. If we cannot find a location for a residing thought, that means it is devoid of a real nature. Finally, if we cannot find a place where thoughts go, that means there is no result. So we have the nonexistence of a cause, being devoid of any real existence, and the absence of a result. These three comprise the second mental activity, discriminating examination.

The third of the eleven mental actions is called *detailed analysis*. In thorough searching and discriminating examination, we look at the mind and are not able to find any truly existent object. In detailed analysis, we look to see what it is that has been searching—the searcher itself. We look at the subject rather than the object. We look and see that it has no real existence. We do all these examinations because previously we had the belief that the mind existed, like matter. Even if we look at the nature of mind and cannot find anything, that negative tendency still remains. Therefore, by doing this detailed analysis again and again, we will gradually eliminate the negative tendency of seeing the mind as having a real existence.

The fourth mental activity is called *shamatha*, but this is not the usual shamatha. This is the shamatha that arises from vipashyana, a peace and stability that comes through insight. The previous mental activities were search, examination, and analysis. First, we search in order to find the mind as a thing, as an entity, and we find that it has no real nature. Then through examination, we try to find where thoughts arise from, where they stay, and where they go, but we cannot find any place. In analysis we look at the mind itself, the mind that searches and examines, but cannot find that either; instead, we see that it is devoid of any reality. The reason we cannot find anything is not that we have failed in our search or don't know how to look but that the mind has no real nature of its own. When we have searched, examined, and analyzed and have seen that the mind has no real nature, we can comprehend this meaning without being distracted by anything else: When we see something, the seer is the mind; when we think something, the thinker is the mind. Whatever arises, it is just the mind. Thus, we remain in this profound meaning without distraction, and this brings a definite certainty. This is what is meant here by the mental activity of shamatha, or peaceful stability.

The empty nature of the mind is not a material emptiness. In the Tibetan tradition, a material emptiness is said to be like a corpse or like empty space. In empty space there are no positive qualities or anything else—it is just plain empty. The empty nature of mind is not a material vacuity, like the lifelessness of a corpse, because it has the knowing of the empty nature. There is a knowing, and the nature of that knowing itself is empty. When we say "emptiness," the Sanskrit term is *shunyata*. Shunyata can be followed by the word *jñana*, which means wisdom: thus, *shunyata jñana*. There is emptiness, but there is also the knowledge of emptiness, and that knowledge itself is empty. Resting in that state is the fourth mental activity, shamatha. Shamatha in this context means to rest in the state of emptiness and knowing.

The fifth mental activity is called *vipashyana*, or insight. Here, what is specifically meant by this term is that as a result of the previous mental activities, one has reached a state of stability in terms of understanding. Now, with the same kind of looking as in the previous mental activities, one looks at the nature of that stability and gains a complete realization of its nature. One gains a state of clarity concerning the stability of realization.

The sixth mental activity is called *union*. This means that all the previous mental activities are not separate mental activities. They are all one. For a beginner, shamatha and vipashyana are two separate meditations, but now they are not distinct from each other. So the sixth mental activity is the union of all the previous five mental activities.

Clarity, the seventh mental activity, concerns the arising of dullness in meditation. Whether one is practicing shamatha or vipashyana meditation, sometimes a state of dullness can arise. This is eliminated by encouraging oneself through thinking how fortunate one is. The seventh mental activity is refreshing and brightening the mind in order to eliminate any dullness.

Brightening or energizing the mind can lead to a state of agitation and instability, with many thoughts arising. Therefore, one also needs a method to pacify and bring contentment to the mind. This means entering a state in which few thoughts arise, and this is the eighth mental activity: *nonthought*. When there is agitation and instability, and the mind has too many thoughts, the remedy as described earlier is to develop a sense of sadness. Both dullness and agitation can be eliminated by remedies, and one obtains the seventh and eighth states of clarity and nonthought as a result of dispelling these obstacles.

The ninth mental activity is *equanimity*. When one has eliminated dullness and agitation, one can remain in a state of equanimity. One simply rests in that state in which one is looking at the nature of the mind, free of dullness and agitation.

There may be periods of time when one sees the nature of the mind, but then at other times one completely forgets. With mindfulness and awareness, one can maintain the continuous awareness of the nature of the mind. This is the tenth mental activity: *continuity*. This means that throughout one's meditation sessions or postmeditation periods, one's meditation is as continuous as the flow of a river. One doesn't have strict meditation sessions followed by postmeditation periods of no longer paying any attention to meditation. Instead, one maintains a continuity of meditation at all times.

The eleventh mental activity is *nondistraction*. This means that as a result of mindfulness and awareness, one's mind is always in meditation and is never distracted. Distractions are often able to find opportunities to bring the mind out of meditation, but now, because of mindfulness and awareness, one's meditation is never disturbed or destroyed by distraction.

An Ocean of the Ultimate Meaning states that while these eleven mental activities can be understood in a conceptual manner, and while such an understanding is good, it will not accomplish the results we seek in meditation. Therefore, these activities should be put into practice during meditation sessions and also between sessions, when there are many things that can act as distractions and cause us to lose our meditation. Instead, we need to control the mind during postmeditation periods so that we can maintain the meditation continuously.

IX

Developing Certainty in the Union of Emptiness and Awareness

Typically, the mind is focused outward; we don't look in at the nature of the mind. In Mahamudra practice, however, we look in at the nature of the mind. This Mahamudra way of looking at the mind is different from the usual way in which we have observed the mind, and therefore it can be difficult to do. We are usually in a state of delusion, experiencing illusory appearances and not seeing the mind's nature. In order to eliminate this state of delusion, we need to look at the mind in a state of stability and see its true nature. This is what we do in insight meditation.

There are three parts to this process. The first is looking at the nature of the mind in a state of stability. The second is cutting through the root, so as to gain certainty in the nature of the mind. The third part is the certainty in awareness and emptiness. In Tibetan, awareness and emptiness are called *rigtong*. *Tong* means empty. When one looks at the nature of the mind, there is nothing that has real existence; it's empty. But that doesn't mean that it's nothing whatsoever, that it is a state of darkness or oblivion. As well as *tong*, or emptiness, there is *rig*, awareness. There is an awareness, a knowing. So although there is this clarity, this knowing and awareness, if one looks to see *who* is being aware, *who* is knowing, one can't find anything that has any reality. One finds nothing that has a nature of its own. Therefore, there is a union of awareness and emptiness.

Then one thinks, "Where is the mind located?" There are different viewpoints. Some people think the mind is located in the heart; others, that it is located in the brain. Also, one considers the six consciousnesses, which are said to be in different locations. However, the nature of the mind and consciousness is emptiness, and this expanse of emptiness is permeated by knowing, or *rigpa*. This knowing, or awareness, is said to be all-pervasive. It pervades the entirety of emptiness, which is the nature of the mind. Therefore, the mind cannot be said to have any location.

In realizing this nature, because of the different kinds of minds that people have and the different conditions of their *nadis* and the airs that move through them, people have different kinds of meditation. There are said to be, in general, three different types of meditators.

The first is the immediate type. Just by supplicating the teacher, hearing some teachings, or seeing some kind of sign, meditators of this type immediately experience the nature of the mind. Or it can happen that just by doing a little meditation these meditators immediately have an experience. Experiences can be of various kinds, higher or lower, but they appear to this type of meditator very quickly.

The second kind of meditator is nonconsecutive. Rather than progressing steadily stage by stage, they jump from stage to stage. One such meditator may develop good insight without having shamatha, or another may achieve shamatha without having developed insight. Such meditators may sometimes have good and sometimes bad experiences. These first two types, the immediate practitioner and the nonconsecutive type, are both unpredictable. The development of their practice does not take a normal route.

The third kind of practitioner is the gradual type. These meditators progress step by step through the stages of meditation. Beginning without much experience or realization, they first develop shamatha meditation, and then they develop vipashyana. In accordance with the consecutive levels, they develop meditation, experience, and realization. This is a very stable and definite development that is predictable, unlike the other two types.

An Ocean of the Ultimate Meaning presents the teachings in terms of the gradual practitioner because only a few people are the immediate or nonconsecutive kinds of practitioners. Most people are the gradual, progressive type. However, this text is useful for the first two types as well because it is beneficial for everyone to know the progressive order in which experience and realization develop.

In the gradual approach, it is taught that one should develop faith and devotion to the guru and the Three Jewels and pray to them. For example, one recites the Vajradhara Mahamudra lineage prayer, in which it states that devotion is the head of meditation. With faith and devotion, one then meditates free of distraction and obstacles, with the mind resting in a relaxed state, whether in shamatha or in vipashyana, within the certainty one has gained from seeing the nature of the mind.

Rest the mind in a state of natural relaxation, that is, not tense or tight. You are not controlling the mind; it is simply in a natural state of rest. In this relaxed state, look nakedly and vividly at the nature of the relaxed mind. "Nakedly" means uncovered, as if one has removed an obscuring layer. What does it mean to say that something is obscured by a covering? There are two ways of gaining knowledge: directly or through inference. Through the latter approach, one gains a conceptual understanding. One thinks, "Ah, yes, this is the way it is." But this is not the same as seeing the true nature. Instead, it is like seeing the external skin. Meditation should be free from conceptualization, so that the outer covering does not obscure the true nature. One should see the essence of the relaxed mind nakedly and vividly, which means with clarity.

This is the first aspect of the meditation: seeing the nature of the mind nakedly and vividly. A second aspect is maintaining a continuity of mindfulness. One always needs mindfulness in one's meditation; one should not allow mindfulness to diminish or be lost. There are two ways that one can be loose and relaxed in meditation. One can be relaxed yet undistracted, or one can be relaxed while following whatever thought arises in the mind. In this context, a relaxed meditation means maintaining a continuum of mindfulness all the time. This mindfulness is not forced; it is a light mindfulness that simply does not forget the meditation and become distracted. It is this remembering that primarily maintains the continuity of meditation in a relaxed state.

The third characteristic of the meditation is that whatever thought arises, you do not eliminate it, cultivate it, or make any kind of correction to it. You don't think, "This is a bad thought and should be eliminated," or "This is a good thought that I should have." You don't try to make any kind of change to the meditation. Instead, just look at the nature of the thought, and it will naturally disappear by itself. Whatever thoughts arise, don't try to eliminate, cultivate, or change anything; just look at the true nature. The clarity and emptiness of the mind will then be seen directly, nakedly. Don't try to look for something new that isn't in the mind or create something new that is not already there. Just look directly at the nature of the mind. That is the third characteristic of this meditation.

The main point is to maintain a continuity of meditation and have just the right degree of mindfulness necessary to maintain it. The teacher Gyalwa Yanggönpa said that in meditation one does not identify the mind as being anything—existent, nonexistent, empty, or not empty. As a result of not identifying the mind as anything, one rests within the expanse of emptiness. Emptiness is the nature of the mind, which also has clarity. Thus, there is an awareness that is the union of clarity and emptiness. The meditation consists of resting the mind in itself exactly as it is, without thinking in terms of existence or nonexistence or anything else—just resting in the mind as it is while looking at the mind itself. If you can do that, Yanggönpa says, you will see the true face of vipashyana. That is true insight meditation.

But meditation can also be artificial. In this case, we have not realized the nature of the mind, and we have not seen the emptiness, yet we think that we have. We think, "In my meditation, I see the empty nature of the mind. I have clarity; I have emptiness in my meditation." But this is just an artificial meditation, not genuinely seeing the nature of the mind.

Similarly, meditation can be merely a conceptual understanding. Through reasoning we arrive at the conclusion that the nature of the mind is emptiness because it has no shape, no color, and so on. This is a conceptual knowledge that comes from learning and contemplation. It is an externally directed wisdom; it is not a direct experience of the nature of the mind. The wisdom that comes from learning and contemplation is good. The conceptual understanding that the nature of phenomena is empty and therefore the nature of the mind is also empty can be the cause for the eventual realization of the emptiness of the mind. But this conceptual wisdom isn't true meditation. In meditation we need the direct experience of the nature of the mind, the emptiness of the mind, which is not fabricated and is not a conceptual understanding.

In meditation, one can have experience, and one can have conceptual understanding. Sometimes it is easy to differentiate between the two, but sometimes they are mixed so that one mistakes conceptual understanding for experience. One also needs to distinguish between experiences and realizations. There are three things that one can have: conceptual understanding, experiences, and realizations. To have a conceptual understanding of something is good, but better than that is to attain an experience. In meditation, one can have good experiences, lesser experiences, and so on, but what is even more important than these is the realization of the true nature of the mind. Realization is the most important, so one should not have attachment to experiences.

If we think we have had an experience, we need to examine it very carefully to see whether it was genuine. When we investigate in vipashyana meditation, we may come to the conclusion that nothing new has been seen, that we have not seen anything that we haven't seen before. This is a sign that we need to continue with the practice.

When we meditate on thoughts as they arise, we may find nothing that we can identify—there is just nothing whatsoever. Wangchuk Dorje says that in this case the meditator has partial insight. It is partial in that we see the emptiness aspect of the mind, but we do not have the experience of clarity. Therefore, the meditator needs to continue with the practice of vipashyana. Look at the emptiness of mind that has been seen. Is it simply an emptiness like empty space? Or does it have a special quality? Examine the emptiness in that way.

The meditator may not find anything identifiable in meditation—no thing, no entity, no matter. But in addition, a vivid, clear, naked clarity is continuously present: There is a knowing. Although there is nothing to be found or identified in the mind, there is still this knowing quality, a continuous ability at all times and in all situations to know. This is an experience that for the meditator is beyond words and beyond thought. In describing the perfection of wisdom the Buddha said that it is indescribable and inconceivable. It is beyond the conceptual understanding of the mind. Its nature is empty and like space. But what is it that knows this emptiness, this nature of the mind? It is the self-knowing wisdom, the mind that knows itself. Self-knowing wisdom sees this nature of the mind, which cannot be put into words or thoughts. It is purely the experience of self-knowing, the knowing that knows itself.

With conceptual understanding, we establish that the nature of the mind has neither arising nor ceasing. But the direct experience in meditation is beyond any *idea* of existence or nonexistence. It is a direct experience of the nature of the mind as it is. This is called the union of knowledge and emptiness because clarity is present along with the understanding of emptiness. This is the union of knowledge, or knowing, with emptiness.

We can have this experience in a state without thought, in

shamatha. Then when a thought arises, we look at that thought to see how it arises, where it is, and where it goes. Thus, we can have a direct experience of the nature of that thought. In terms of its appearance or essence, there is nothing we can find or identify. We gain an understanding of emptiness, of the nature of thought and the nature of the mind, but there is a knowing, so it's not merely emptiness. There is clarity in the direct experience.

Conceptual understanding is not stable or enduring, but the understanding that is gained through experience is. When we see that there's nothing there, this is not a state of darkness. There is a continuing clarity and awareness.

The phrase "liberation through arising" means the liberation of thoughts as they arise. This does not mean that we stop all thought; doing so would not be genuine meditation. Rather, it refers to seeing the nature of thought. We experience the nature of thought and see that there is nothing there. This is liberation through arising. In this way, we gain genuine realization through meditation. That is the union of clarity and emptiness.

The way we attain this genuine realization is by first practicing shamatha meditation and then, within that shamatha, developing vipashyana. We look at the essence of the meditation and see that the essence of the mind has no reality, and that is self-knowing wisdom. But in order to gain this realization, we have to look at the essence of the meditation. If we do not, we will not see the essence of the mind and there will be no self-knowing knowledge, and thus no realization.[1]

Sometimes in meditation we can have an experience of clarity that subsequently vanishes. The experience is not stable—sometimes it's there and sometimes not. This means that we need to dedicate ourselves to our meditation with diligence.

All the great masters have said that we need mindfulness and awareness in shamatha in order to maintain and develop the meditation. The same is true of vipashyana—with mindfulness and awareness we will be able to maintain and develop it. Dakpo Tashi

Namgyal said that in order to maintain the continuity of meditation, one's mindfulness needs to be very clear and sharp. He said that the nature of the mind is innate; that nature has always been emptiness and clarity, and it has always been there. We just haven't recognized it. The nature of the mind is not something we have to create or something new that we have to obtain. It is primordial, and if we recognize it, we will think, "Ah, yes! This has always been here."

POINTING OUT THE NATURE OF MIND THROUGH MOVEMENT

In talking about this innateness of the mind, Dakpo Tashi Namgyal was referring to meditation on the mind in stillness. In relation to meditation on the mind in movement, when thoughts are arising, Dakpo Tashi Namgyal spoke about this innateness within thought. When the mind is in a state of stillness, we can generate a thought in order to look at its nature. Whether it is the thought of a house, or a place of amusement, or a car, when we generate this thought and look at its nature, we see that it's empty. If we compare the mind in stillness with the mind in movement, we see that their nature is the same: They are both empty. The mind in stillness and the mind in movement are different from each other, but when we look at the nature of the mind in these two states, we find that their nature is the same.

For example, we may have a thought of a Mercedes. When we think of a Mercedes, a Mercedes will appear to the mind. We look at this Mercedes and ask, "Where did this Mercedes-thought come from? Where does it reside?" We will not find anything. When we look at the Mercedes, we find that the nature of this Mercedes-thought is empty. It is the same for all thoughts that arise. When we look at them, we can't find where they came from, where they are, or where they go.

If we have many thoughts, we might think, "I have too many

thoughts! I have to get rid of them!" If we think in that way, our thoughts will become the enemies of our meditation. When we look at the nature of the thoughts, they become the focus of our meditation instead of its enemy. Generally, thoughts are harmful to meditation, but we can make thoughts the focus of our meditation instead, which is beneficial.

In looking at the mind in movement—whether it is already in movement or we cause it to be in movement—our intention is to recognize its nature. Generally, the state of stillness and the state of movement appear to be two distinct things. The movement of the mind is seen as a disruption or an obstacle to the stillness of the mind, and that is exactly what it is. But here, when movement occurs, instead of trying to stop it, we look at the thought in order to recognize the nature of the movement of the mind.

For example, we look at happiness and unhappiness, which seem to be two very different things. We think of something that we like—a person we like, or a food—so that we generate a feeling of happiness in thinking, "I really like that person; I really like this food." We can think of things we don't like and develop a feeling of unhappiness. We then look at these feelings of happiness and unhappiness to see what they are like: What is this happiness like? How does it arise? What is this unhappiness? What is it like? How does it arise? Where does this happiness or unhappiness arise from, where is it present, where does it cease, and where does it go? By looking at them both, we find that both happiness and unhappiness are by nature empty. There is nothing that can be found or identified. They may seem to be two distinct things, but if we look into them, we can't find anything real that differentiates them.

When a thought arises in the mind, look directly at its essence. Look *nakedly* at that thought to see: What is that thought? Where is it arising? How is it arising? Where is it? How does it cease? Look directly at whatever arises and you will find that there is nothing to be found. The thought has no real nature of its own. You can't find any place where it arises from, where it is, or where it goes. You can't say, "The thought is here," or "The thought is there," or "The thought is this thing." You see that it is empty of any nature.

Realizing the empty nature of this thought is the union of clarity and emptiness. When you see the essence of a thought and see that it is devoid of any nature, that thought is liberated. You can do this with any thought that arises in the mind. Negative thoughts—of anger, jealousy, miserliness, and so on—may arise in the mind, and one would normally think that these are bad and would seek to eliminate them. But that is unnecessary: Just look at the nature of the bad thought, and by seeing that it has no nature of its own, one is liberated from it. Thus, thoughts are spontaneously liberated. If you were trying to eliminate them, you would have to apply a remedy, but in this practice there is no need for any remedy other than looking directly at the nature of the thought itself. Look at the thought to see what it is, where it is, where it comes from—and nothing is found.

It was said by one of the siddhas, "By knowing what binds us, we will be liberated." There are different things that bind us, but we don't need to cut through that bondage. We only need to know the nature of that bondage, and then we will be liberated. An old example likens this to a snake that has been tied in a knot and then unravels itself. If we can see the nature of what binds us, we are liberated, and by using this special path we can attain buddhahood in one lifetime.

In addition to looking at happiness and unhappiness, you can look at the kleshas, the defilements. By thinking about something that you feel is pleasant and toward which you feel attachment, you can de-velop a strong desire for it, so that you have no control over the feeling of attachment. You should then look at that feeling of desire to see what its source is, what its essence is, and so on. When you do this, you will not be able to find any essence. You will see that it is empty. Similarly, you can think of something unpleasant, such as an enemy who has been harmful, and then develop strong anger.[2] You then look at this anger to see what its source is, what its essence is, and so on. Again, you can find no real essence to it.

Concerning this, Ratna Lingpa has said that the essence of anger is very clear awareness; there is a great deal of clarity within anger. By looking at the essence of that anger, you will see that it has no real essence. Do this with attachment, anger, and other defilements like pride and envy. You may feel pride, thinking, "I am so much better than everyone else." You may feel envy toward another or have covetous thoughts toward someone's possessions. When these strong feelings arise, look into their essence to see where they've come from, where they are, what their essence is, and you will not find any essence to them. When you have seen this empty nature, rest within that and maintain that state of resting through mindfulness.

When a thought has arisen and you have seen its nature, there is an immediate discontinuity of thought. So when anger, envy, and so on arise and you see their empty nature, rest in it with mindfulness. There should not be a continuation in terms of another defilement arising. If thoughts continue to come, they will be an obstacle to your meditation. You should be able to rest in the empty nature of the thought without any continuity of that kind of thought.

It is said that looking for just a short time at the empty essence of desire, anger, and so on will not be beneficial. In order to recognize the empty nature of these kinds of thoughts, one has to do this for a long time. For example, *An Ocean of the Ultimate Meaning* says that one should do ten sessions on thoughts of desire, ten on anger, ten on envy, ten on pride, ten on miserliness, and so on. One looks into the essence of these thoughts, not with laziness but with a sharp clarity so that there will be certainty in the recognition that occurs in the meditation.

Defilements—thoughts of desire, anger, envy, pride, and so on— will also arise in postmeditation. Whatever thoughts arise, do not become involved with them. Instead, look directly and nakedly into the nature of the thoughts and see that they are empty of any real nature. You will then recognize that which was already empty of any reality as being empty of any reality. As we saw earlier, the recognition of the empty nature of thoughts frees us from them. We are naturally liberated from the thoughts, so that there is no need to eliminate them by any other method. Simply seeing that they are devoid of any reality frees us from defiled thoughts. Having seen the thought's nature, rest within it, without any distraction. Thus, when thoughts of desire or anger arise, we don't need to eliminate them. They will be spontaneously liberated, or self-liberated, through our seeing their empty nature. If we see and are attached to thoughts as being real, then it will be very difficult to be free from them. But by our seeing that their nature is empty, then thoughts are self-liberated.

This is called "the five poisons transformed into the path." Generally speaking, the five mind poisons are to be eliminated. But in this path of Mahamudra, they are self-liberated through our seeing their empty nature, without the need to use remedies to eliminate them. This meditation is a view of the mind in movement. It can also be called "transforming thought into the path" or "adopting the five poisons as the path." It is a superior instruction through which, without the need to use remedies, there is liberation by means of seeing the empty nature.

We can do this. We *can* see the nature of defilements as they arise. It is easy to have merely a conceptual understanding and then to think that we are looking at the nature of the defilements. But through meditation one will progress. At first, when the defilements are very strong and we are habituated to them, it will be difficult to have the experience of seeing their nature. By continuing with the practice, however, we can definitely gain the experience of seeing the nature of the defilements.

Having adopted the defilements as the path, we are instructed next to look at the nature of *all* thoughts—good or bad, big or small—and see that their nature is the same: devoid of reality. Again, no other remedy is necessary. When we see the nature of any thought or feeling, that thought or feeling is liberated. We cultivate this seeing during all our activities: going, staying, eating, sleeping, suffering, worrying, and so on. No other remedy is necessary.

Speaking of this, Gampopa said that thoughts are actually the *dharmakaya*; they are empty, devoid of reality, and therefore they are not the obstacles we normally think them to be. We don't need to apply any kind of correction; we simply remain in the clarity of knowing emptiness. Whatever thought arises, its nature is emptiness, and when that is seen and the thought dissolves, we rest in that. Thoughts may cease, but there is still the clarity that accompanies emptiness.

Maitreyanatha taught in the *Uttaratantra Shastra* that there is nothing to be eliminated and nothing to be added. The nature of mind and thoughts is already the true nature, and if one can see this nature, there is liberation.

Gampopa said that thoughts should be viewed as necessary, having great kindness, beloved, and indispensable. Thoughts are necessary because we want to see the true nature of phenomena, and we are able to do this by looking at thoughts. Thoughts are kind because without seeing the true nature of mind, we wander in samsara. It is hard to see the true nature of mind by looking outward at phenomena, but we can accomplish this by looking at thoughts. If we can see the nature of thoughts, this is the essence of practice and is beneficial. For this reason, thoughts are beloved. If we see thoughts as bad, then when a thought arises, we will have to stop it, and when another arises, we will have to stop that one, too. But this is difficult. If, however, we recognize the true nature of thoughts, then there will be no obstacle or difficulty. Therefore, thoughts are indispensable.

An Ocean of the Ultimate Meaning describes three mistaken ways of viewing thoughts. First, one might come to the conclusion that there are no thoughts. This is incorrect. There are thoughts—they do exist—but they are empty. If one comes to that mistaken conclusion, one should continue with the meditation on viewing the nature of thoughts.

Second, someone might say, "Thoughts are empty," or "Thoughts are beyond all concepts," but simply speaking such words is not beneficial. It's not enough just to say thoughts are empty—we have to realize this. We need to look directly at the thoughts themselves and generate experience in meditation.

Finally, a person may be learned and scholarly and know many quotations, but these are just words and of no use here. What is useful is to look at the nature of the thoughts themselves. Many types of thoughts can arise in meditation—thoughts of a friend, thoughts of an enemy, thoughts of happiness, thoughts of suffering, and so on. The point is to identify all of them as simply created by the mind.

POINTING OUT THE NATURE OF MIND THROUGH APPEARANCES

There are three ways in which one can directly recognize the nature of the mind: through stillness, through movement, and through appearances. In another teaching, five ways are presented, but *An Ocean of the Ultimate Meaning* presents three. If one recognizes the nature of mind using any one of these approaches, it is all-inclusive: One has recognized all three. If, however, one is not able to recognize the mind's nature through one method, then one can move on to another.

The third method is direct introduction by way of appearances. This is gained through experience, not by reasoning, but I have found that it is beneficial if one first has a conceptual understanding of the way in which appearances are not other than mind. With this understanding, one can gradually develop the actual experience of appearances as mind. Therefore, I will explain the philosophical tradition of the sutras that establishes how appearances do not go beyond mind.

Philosophical Explanations of Appearances as Mind

The Buddha taught beginners that externally there are appearances and internally there is the mind. This initial teaching is in accord with the way things appear to be. In other sutras, the Buddha taught a more profound meaning: that external phenomena have no reality and are nothing other than mind.

After the Buddha's nirvana, great scholars presented the teachings in a definitive form. Arhats taught the lesser yana, the Hinayana, and bodhisattvas transmitted the Mahayana. Then there arose four philosophical traditions: the Vaibhashika, the Sautrantika, the Chittamatra, and the Madhyamaka. The first two, the Vaibhashika and Sautrantika, belong to the Hinayana. The Chittamatra (Mind Only) and Madhyamaka (Middle Way) schools belong to the Mahayana.

THE HINAYANA VIEWS

The two schools of the Hinayana tradition are the Vaibhashika (the followers of the Vibhasha text) and the Sautrantika (the followers of the sutras). Both schools stated that there is a subject that perceives and that there are external objects that are perceived—that is, both the subject and the external object truly exist.

The Vaibhashikas and Sautrantikas held that even though there are external existents, objects, such as mountains, are mere conceptual designations and have no true existence because they are actually an aggregation of smaller parts. A mountain that one perceives is actually a collection of smaller and smaller constituents. Thus, there is really no such thing as a mountain; it does not exist as an independent entity. The same is true of all external objects.

According to the Vaibhashikas and the Sautrantikas, objects are made up of atoms: very small, truly existing, indivisible particles. It is from the combination of these indivisible particles that all phenomena are formed. These schools go on to say that even though all phenomena on their obvious level have no real existence, the indivisible particles that comprise them do exist.

The teaching of the Vaibhashikas and the Sautrantikas accords with the way things appear to be, so it is easy to understand. You have a mind on the inside and objects of perception on the outside, and the mind perceives those objects of perception. In general, that is their teaching, though there are some specific differences between these two traditions.

The Vaibhashikas stated that, just as people normally think, there is an inner mind and there are external objects, and the mind perceives these objects. Perception occurs in each instant; a present consciousness perceives a present object of perception moment by moment. The object of perception itself is seen by the consciousness of that moment. This is the view of the Vaibhashika, in which external objects have their own reality, their own nature.

The Sautrantikas held a different view. They said that the mind is an awareness, a clear knowing, whereas external phenomena are inert matter made of atoms. This awareness and this inert matter are different entities that cannot connect with each other. How then does one perceive an external object? This has to operate according to the law of causation, of cause and result. The Sautrantikas believed that the external object is the cause and the perceiving consciousness is the result. When there is a cause-and-result relationship, the two components—in this case, the consciousness and the object—cannot exist at the same time. When there is a cause present, the result cannot be present in that same instant; when there is a result, the cause is no longer present. Thus, the consciousness cannot perceive the external object directly because a cause and result cannot coexist.

The Sautrantikas taught that when you see a mountain, both the external object and the sensory faculty are present. The mountain functions as the cause, and in the next instant there is a visual consciousness that perceives the mountain. However, the consciousness does not perceive the actual mountain; instead, in that subsequent instant, the consciousness experiences the *appearance* of a mountain. Thus, the Sautrantikas stated that there is a cause-and-result relationship between outer perceived objects and the inner mind.

According to the Sautrantikas, the sensory consciousness takes on the form of the external object; it does not perceive the external object itself. For example, if we look at a glass of water, we don't actually see the glass itself; instead, our visual consciousness takes on the form of the glass in each successive instant. In each instant, the object of perception creates a subsequent instant of a consciousness. Thus, according to the Sautrantikas, when we perceive, we do not perceive the actual external object; we perceive the form taken on by the sensory consciousness. In denying that we perceive the actual external object, the Sautrantikas asserted that we perceive something that arises in our own mind.

For example, when we look at a mirror, a reflection appears, but what we see is not actually in the mirror. Rather, our form is a cause, which has resulted in the reflection appearing in the mirror. That object is not actually in the mirror; it is a result, and our form is the cause. The Sautrantikas taught that when we perceive something, we are not perceiving the actual object itself but an appearance that arises in our own mind as a result of the external object.

Both the Vaibhashikas and the Sautrantikas held that there are externally existing objects, but the latter believed that the mind experiences only their appearance.

THE MIND ONLY VIEW

The Chittamatra school agreed that the mind experiences appearances; however, the Chittamatrins disagreed with the Vaibhashikas and the Sautrantikas concerning the existence of an external object. The Chittamatrins said that there are no external objects that can act as causes for the perception of appearances.

The Hinayana views stated that when we have a perception, that perception is either of or caused by an actual external object that is composed of atoms. The Chittamatra school, on the other hand, said that these atoms do not exist. According to the Chittamatrins, even the smallest particle would have to have a front and a back, a top and a bottom, sides, and a middle. Therefore, it is a divisible, not an indivisible particle and is merely a conceptual designation. The indivisible particle has no real existence, and so external phenomena have no reality. Therefore, there are no real external objects that can serve as causes for mental appearances.

How then, according to the Chittamatrins, do appearances arise? They held that the perceived object and the mind are, in essence, one and the same. The Chittamatrins gave two reasons for asserting that appearances are the same as the mind. The first reason is related with the clarity and knowing quality of the mind. What is it that perceives objects? It is the mind, for there is nothing else that can perceive. If you see a mountain, what is the mountain? It is the mind. Nothing else can perceive, nothing else can understand, nothing else can know. It is solely the mind that perceives objects. This is the first reason that the mind and objects are one: They have the same nature.

The second reason is the mind's togetherness with the object. If two things are separate, they are not the same—sometimes you'll see them together and sometimes not. For example, two people are different, so sometimes you may see them together, but sometimes they'll be apart and you'll see them singly. But the object of perception and the perceiver are always together. In the perception of a mountain, for example, there are both the subject and the object. You can never have an object of perception without a subject, and you can never have a perceiver without an object of perception. You never have a subject by itself, that is, without an object. These two things are always found together. This is because they are the same thing, which is why they are always together. Therefore, appearances and the mind are the same.

Thus, one can establish through reasoning that appearances are the mind and that they have no external existence. Yet because we are habituated to the idea of there being external objects, we still find it difficult to accept. We think, "There *must* be external objects. It's impossible to have these perceptions or appearances without there being something existing externally." But in fact, it is possible, as in dreams. Things like mountains and houses appear in our dreams, but there is really nothing there. Even though there is nothing, appearances still occur as if there is something. In the same way, the Chittamatrins claimed, the mind manifests all of our sensory perceptions. Nonexistent things appear as if they do exist, but they are just the appearances of the mind. The mind itself takes on the form of an object of perception, but there is no external object composed of material atoms that acts as a cause. Thus, it is possible for there to be perceptions without the existence of an external object. In this way, the Chittamatrins established through reasoning that perceptions are mental appearances, that appearances are the mind.

Recognition through Direct Experience

We have looked at the recognition of the mind in stillness and the recognition of the mind in movement. In the recognition of the mind on the basis of appearances, first we see that there is nothing other than the mind; then we see that the mind itself is empty of any nature of its own. Third, we see that although the mind is empty, there is the natural presence of the arising of the variety of all things. Fourth, we recognize this natural presence as being self-liberated.

POINTING OUT THAT APPEARANCES ARE MIND

Having established through reasoning the nonexistence of external phenomena and that appearances are not other than mind, *An Ocean of the Ultimate Meaning* gives instructions on how to gain this understanding through experience. If there is an object before you that you can see clearly, focus your eyes and mind on it. Keep looking at it. After some time passes, you will want to stop looking at this object; if you keep looking, you will eventually experience some physical discomfort in your eyes. While looking at this object, you believe, "I'm seeing this." But what does "seeing" mean? What is seeing? What is it that perceives the object? An appearance arises in your perception, and you look to see exactly what it is. Is it something that exists separately from the mind? By looking in this way, you will understand that the object is an appearance arising in your own consciousness and has no existence apart from your own mind.

While looking at an object, we usually think, "I'm looking at an external object. My mind is internal and is now seeing that external object." That thought naturally arises because we are so used to that perspective. For example, as you look at a glass of water, you think, "This glass is appearing to my visual consciousness." But where is this visual consciousness? Is it in the eyes? When it perceives the glass, how far does this visual consciousness extend? Is it just in the eyes, or does it come out, say, halfway to the glass? Does it come all the way out until it touches the glass? Does your mind cover the glass completely? Stare at the glass and keep trying to determine how far the visual consciousness extends. Does it just go as far as the side you can see, or does it extend to the other side of the glass? You will find no point to which the visual consciousness extends. As a result, you will come to the understanding that the perception of the glass is simply an appearance arising within the mind.

Then you might think, "This glass is an appearance within my mind, without there being any external object, yet it appears as an external object. But what does that mean? Is it my mind that goes out to form the glass? Or is it that the glass has come into my mind?" Look at the visual object and examine how you actually see it. How does this "seeing" occur? Do the same with sound and your ears. Observe what happens. Does the sound have to come into your ears in order to become the consciousness that perceives sound? Or does the consciousness go out and become the sound?

In the same way, examine smell, taste, and touch to see how these perceptions actually occur. The Buddha taught in the sutras that all the three realms are nothing other than mind. On the one hand, there are appearances that arise to our visual consciousness, but as well, some things appear that are just mental fabrications. For example, when we see a flower with our visual consciousness, we think, "This is a flower." In Tibetan the word for flower is *metok*. We see the object, and then we say the two syllables *me* and *tok*, or *flow* and *er*. The word "flower" doesn't actually exist in the object that we see. There's no reason that we say *flow-* and there's no reason that we say *-er*. Nevertheless, we look at that object, and we think "flower," even though there's really no flower there. Yet we look at a flower and think, "This is a flower; it's red." In Tibetan the word "red" is *marpo,* but there's no *mar* or *po* in the flower, just as there's no *re-* or *-d.* We see "red," we see "green," we see "flower," but all of these are just created by the mind: There's no *flow-er,* no *re-d,* and no *gr-een* there. These are just creations of the mind. By examining perceptions, we gain a certainty that objects have no real external existence, that they are just the appearances of the mind.

Next, we look inward at the body to see if it is other than mind. We tend to think of the body as being other than the mind. We think of the body as a sort of house, and the mind as a person dwelling inside that house. But we need to examine our presumed perception.

If we are pricked with a needle in the head or the foot, there will be pain. There is an experience of pain and an experiencer that feels pain. But who is experiencing that pain? Is it the mind or the body? The body is made of matter, as is a table. If you stick a needle in a table, you don't feel anything, but if you stick a needle in your body, it hurts. If the mind and body are separate things, why should that occur? It must be that the mind is the one experiencing the pain. But if you conclude that it is the mind that experiences that pain, how do you stick a needle in the mind? The mind is merely awareness, so how can you stick a needle into it?

Look at the body and examine how the body is the body and how the mind is the mind. Look for the boundary between the mind and the body, and you will not find any difference between them. They are the same. You will not find any difference between the body and the mind because the body is an appearance of the mind.

Seeing appearances and perceptions as being no other than mind is difficult; we are so habituated to thinking of them as not being mind. But by habituating ourselves to this practice and examining repeatedly, we will gain the experience of recognizing appearances as mind.

Gampopa said, "Appearances and mind are one." In our normal way of perceiving, there is the perceived and the perceiver. The perceived are external objects and appearances, and the perceiver is the mind. We usually conceive of these as two; we are attached to the notion of there being both a perceiver and a perceived. Even so, appearances and mind are one. Appearances are the mind. Although we think of appearances as having external existence, they have none, other than being an appearance of the mind. Therefore, appearances are said to be the light, or the true nature, of the mind. Gampopa said that the true nature of the mind, the very mind itself, has the innate quality of being the dharmakaya and that appearances arise from the dharmakaya. The mind is innately the dharmakaya, and all appearances are innately the light that arises from the dharmakaya. This is another way of saying that all appearances are no other than mind.

If we realize the nature of appearances, they are spontaneously liberated. For this reason Tilopa said to Naropa, "Appearances themselves cause no harm; it is the attachment to appearances that binds us. Therefore, my son, do not have attachment."

The true nature of appearances is called *dharmata*, the true nature. We can say that the mind has "mind nature" and that appearances of phenomena have "phenomena nature," but these are not two different things. When one says "the true nature of phenomena" or "the true nature of the mind," these are the same. If one realizes the true nature of the mind, one will realize the true nature of phenomena, the dharmata. If one realizes the true nature of phenomena, one is at the same time realizing the true nature of the mind—they are not different from each other.

It is said that the true nature of phenomena arises from the true nature of mind. Appearances arise from the mind like a light radiating from the true nature of the mind. Gampopa said that these two, the true nature of phenomena and the true nature of mind, are the same. It's like the sun: If you have the sun, you have sunlight. There is no sun without light, and there is no light without the sun. If you have one, then you have the other. It is the same for the true nature of the mind and the true nature of phenomena. If you are able to realize this unity, then you have natural spontaneous liberation.

When we use the term "appearances," we are referring to things that appear as external objects, such as houses and hills. If we look at those external appearances through meditation or by examining them through reasoning, we will find that they are beyond words and thought. Their nature cannot be described through speech or conceived by thought. Their nature is inexpressible.

The true nature of appearances transcends speech or thought because appearances arise from the universal ground, the *alaya,* first as the five sensory faculties, and from these sensory faculties arise sensory consciousnesses and appearances. For example, visual form appears to the eye consciousness, sound appears to the auditory consciousness, smell appears as an object for the nose, taste as an object for the tongue, and touch as an object for the body. Appearances all arise in that way, but their arising is neutral and nonconceptual. But after objects arise to the sensory consciousnesses, there follows the mental consciousness. The mental consciousness reacts, and there arises an inconceivable quantity of internal appearances—distinctions between good and bad, attachment, aversion, and so on. Countless varieties and levels of qualities arise in the mental consciousness— liking and disliking and so on—and all these are also called appearances. So there are the appearances of the sensory objects and the sensory consciousnesses, and also the appearances of the mental consciousness, which makes distinctions between good and bad, liking and disliking, and so on.

If one has attachment to all this, one wanders in samsara. With the arising of appearances, the deluded mind becomes attached to them, and this strong attachment to the vast variety of appearances causes one to be in samsara. Why does this attachment occur? Because of the mind's tendency toward delusion, to which it has been habituated throughout beginningless time. Through the power of this habitual tendency, attachment arises, and we believe that these appearances have a real nature. But if we examine them, we will find they don't have even a sesame seed's worth of reality.

It is helpful to think of appearances as being like dreams. Because of our tendencies created during the day, at night various appearances arise in our dreams. Some dreams can be pleasant, and in some we experience suffering, but all those appearances have no reality. When we wake up, we see that they were unreal. In the same way, through the tendencies created by the deluded mind, appearances arise. They seem to be real, and there seems to be a mind for whom these appearances arise, but these appearances are nothing other than the mind.

As we have seen, the Chittamatra view established that all appearances are no other than mind. The Chittamatrins presented this through logical reasoning, not through direct experience. In the Mahamudra instruction, it is also taught that appearances are no other than mind, but in this case the view comes from the experience of meditation. Basically, both Chittamatra and Mahamudra are teaching the same thing. Therefore, Shantarakshita, in his text *The Adornment of the Middle Way*, says that the tradition of the Chittamatra is a very good one because it teaches that appearances are mind, which is in accord with the Dzogchen and Mahamudra traditions. In the practice of Dzogchen and Mahamudra, one meditates in order to realize directly that all appearances are not other than mind. In Dharma teachings on philosophy, the Chittamatra viewpoint is usually presented as inferior, but it is in fact a very good view in that it establishes that all appearances are nothing other than mind.

So what is wrong with the Chittamatra view? Shantarakshita goes on to say that although the Chittamatrins were correct in stating that all appearances are mind, they erred in conceiving of the mind itself as being an entity. They believed that it has a real existence of its own. In the Dzogchen and Mahamudra traditions, one first establishes that all appearances are mind, and then one goes on to establish that the mind itself is empty. In this way, the Mahamudra teaching is in accord with the Madhyamaka, or Middle Way, tradition.

POINTING OUT THAT MIND IS EMPTY

Next, in accordance with Madhyamaka reasoning, we go on to establish that the mind is empty. We have already established that all appearances are no other than mind. Having recognized this, we will no longer have any attachment to appearances, and consequently, appearances can cause no harm. However, if we still have the delusion that the mind has a real existence, this delusion will be accompanied by attachment. In order to prevent this delusion, we should recognize that the mind, too, is empty. Sometimes it is said that the mind has a natural luminosity, and so forth, but whatever you might call it, it still has no color, form, or shape. The mind, which has the nature of space, is beyond all description and all conception.

In the previous meditations, one had an experience of insight on the basis of the mind in stillness or the mind in movement. The instructions were to search for the mind. One tried to find the mind but couldn't find anything with any reality. One can approach this through analysis by trying to discern the mind's location, color, shape, and so on. Through reasoning, one can establish that the mind has no real existence of its own, but with this approach emptiness becomes something distant that takes a long time to reach. Rather than using reasoning, one can instead gain this realization of emptiness through experience: One meditates on the mind itself. The mind is already available and ready to be meditated upon. By meditating on the mind, one will gain the realization of the nature of the mind and in this way gain the result.

We can always attain this understanding of emptiness through direct meditation on the nature of the mind. We search for the mind, and we are unable to find it. We find no real existence to the mind simply because it has no real nature. It is not that we didn't find the mind because we were looking incorrectly or because we have not yet succeeded in finding it. We will never find it because the mind has no real nature, no true existence.

Since we're unable to see any real nature to the mind, we might say, "Well, if the mind is devoid of any real nature from the beginning, why do we have to look for it? Why go to all the trouble of trying to see whether it has any color, shape, form, and so on?" There is a great purpose in doing this search. Currently, we don't have the realization of the nature of the mind. Because of that lack of realization, we have thoughts that imply a self and "me" and "mine," and we believe that the mind has real existence. Because of this delusion on our part, ignorance, attachment, and aversion arise, and as a result of various thoughts and actions, karma and all the sufferings of samsara are created.

POINTING OUT THAT EMPTINESS IS NATURAL PRESENCE

From our meditation, we need to gain the result. In order to gain that result quickly, we meditate on the mind itself. We might think that by looking at external phenomena, we should be able to realize their true nature. But because of our long-standing habituation to seeing phenomena as real, it is difficult for us to see the true nature of phenomena by looking at external objects.

On the other hand, the mind itself is the embodiment of emptiness, and the only reason we haven't already seen its nature is that we haven't looked at it. It is easier to see the nature of the mind in meditation. We can see that the mind has no real existence, that it does not exist as an entity. Mind is empty, but when one says "empty," this does not mean nonexistent. Rangjung Dorje, the third Karmapa, said in his Mahamudra prayer, "The mind is not existent because even the buddhas have not seen it." It's not because we are mere ordinary beings that we have failed to find a real existence to the mind. Even the buddhas find no real, existing entity when looking at the mind. Therefore, we cannot say that the mind has existence.

So if the mind has no existence, does that mean that it is nonexistent? Rangjung Dorje says, "It is not nonexistent because it is the foundation for all of samsara and nirvana." From beginningless time until now we have been experiencing samsara. What is it that has been experiencing samsara? It is the mind. Therefore, one cannot say that the mind is nonexistent. If one applies oneself to the path and reaches the goal of buddhahood, what is it that achieves buddha-hood? It is the mind. Therefore, one cannot say that the mind is nonexistent, because it is the basis for all of samsara and nirvana. Consequently, the mind is neither existent nor nonexistent.

We usually think of existence and nonexistence as opposites—that is, if something is existent, then it cannot be nonexistent, and if it is nonexistent, then it cannot be existent. For example, if I have a flower in front of me, then the flower is there; it exists. If it is there, it can't not exist. You can see all of its colors and so on. But if the flower is not there, if it is "nonexistent," then it cannot also be right there with all its colors. Therefore, it cannot exist. The two are con-trary to each other. If something does not exist, then it must be non-existent. In the context of the true nature of phenomena, however, these two are not opposites. The path of the Madhyamaka, the Mid-dle Way, speaks of this union of appearance and emptiness, of clarity and emptiness. Something can be not existent and also not nonexis-tent. As this is the true nature of phenomena, there is no contradic-tion. In meditation we should meditate on the true nature in this manner.

When one sees that the mind is empty, this does not mean that it is solely empty, for the mind has a natural presence, the arising of the variety of things.

POINTING OUT THAT NATURAL PRESENCE IS SELF-LIBERATED

The fourth point teaches that the natural presence of the mind is self-liberated. This means that although the nature of mind is empty, all the variety of appearances still arise. Deluded beings wander in sam-sara experiencing all these appearances. One might think that the reason beings are in samsara is the arising of appearances, but that isn't so. Beings wander in samsara because of not having seen the true nature. If one sees the true nature, then one is naturally liberated. In fact, appearances, this essential knowledge, and the empty

nature—or in other words, appearance, knowing, and emptiness—
are primordially united. There is the union of appearance and emptiness, of knowledge and emptiness, and so there is a natural presence,
that is, there is a natural existence of this union of appearance and
emptiness, of knowing and emptiness. All that is necessary is to recognize this natural presence. There are no faults to be eliminated
from nor qualities to be added to this natural, primordial presence.

Natural liberation results from recognizing the natural presence of
the true nature. *An Ocean of the Ultimate Meaning* speaks of "that
which is the cause of being bound." This means that through not
recognizing the nature of the appearances that arise, we have various
thoughts and conceptualizations, and through these we are bound in
samsara. It is this very cause of bondage that is itself the path that
liberates. Recognizing the nature of arising appearances will cause
liberation; it is not that one has to eliminate this arising and find
something new in order to attain liberation. The path that binds is
itself the path that brings liberation.

Meditating on and seeing the nature of the mind is what brings
about liberation. The result is the true, unmistaken wisdom of
vipashyana. Merely having a conceptual understanding that all phenomena are empty—simply thinking that all things are probably
empty—will not be of benefit. A little bit of experience or conceptual understanding will also not bring the necessary accomplishment
of meditation. Instead of a conceptual understanding or a misconception or a fabricated meditation, one needs to develop a genuine, direct experience and view of the nature of the mind. In order to
achieve that result, one must apply oneself to this meditation with
faith, devotion, and diligence.

PART THREE

THE CONCLUDING
TOPICS

X

Enhancing the Result

Once you have received meditation instructions, you need to meditate. If you do only a little meditation and then stop, you won't get the benefits of meditation. Sometimes one can meditate but not make any progress; the following instructions on enhancing the result are intended to remedy this problem. Sometimes one can develop certain faults in meditation, and therefore there are also instructions on removing obstacles. These are the two main points: enhancing the positive results and removing faults and hindrances.

These ancillary points enable one to proceed along the path and gain the result. *An Ocean of the Ultimate Meaning* also gives two additional instructions for progressing further along the path and for attaining the result. Thus, there are actually four points in this conclusion, but the principal points among these four are enhancing the positive results and eliminating obstacles.

ELIMINATING THE FIVE MISCONCEPTIONS

The first set of instructions for enhancing the result is eliminating the five misconceptions. Various misconceptions can arise during practice, and these instructions should be used at such times. The first problem is that while practicing the Dharma, one can develop attachment to adoption and elimination, to cultivation and rejection.

Generally speaking, this is a good thing. One needs to cultivate good qualities and reject the defilements. However, if one has attachment to good deeds without an aspiration to practice meditation, that is a misconception, because cultivation and rejection belong to relative truth, whereas one really needs to realize the true nature of phenomena, the true nature of mind. Avoid the misconception of attachment to adoption and rejection, and apply yourself to meditation on the true nature.

With regard to adoption, it is said in this tradition that the five poisons are to be adopted as the path. Generally speaking, there are three methods in the Buddhist tradition for dealing with the mind poisons: We can eliminate them, transform them, or adopt them as the path. In the Hinayana, the kleshas are eliminated. They are seen as harmful, like poisons, and it is seen as wrong for them to arise. In the Mahayana, the kleshas are transformed. It is as if they are compost—if you add compost to the soil, you get a good harvest. In the Mahayana, one develops relative and ultimate bodhichitta, and through the development of these two bodhichittas the defilements are transformed. In the Mahamudra and Vajrayana, however, the defilements are adopted as the path.

Ordinary beings who do not have any of these methods become involved with the defilements. In the Mahamudra, the harm caused by the defilements is prevented because they are adopted as the path. One looks at their true nature, and as a result, they are self-liberated. This instruction concerns looking at the mind in movement. Thus, when a defilement arises, one should recognize its empty nature, and in this way the defilement is self-liberated. When you adopt the defilements as the path, they become an aid to Mahamudra meditation. If you misunderstand this instruction to mean that you don't have to do anything about the defilements but can instead become involved with them, that will be very harmful. You should neither engage in the defilements nor eliminate them. You shouldn't think of the defilements as something bad that should not arise, but neither should you become involved with them. Instead, when you look at their nature, they are liberated. In this way, the defilements are adopted as the path.

With regard to rejection, what is it that one should reject? In the context of these Mahamudra teachings, one should reject the attitude that sees things as being real, from which follows the habit of adoption and rejection. When you view things as being real, you feel that it is necessary to accomplish something, and so you engage in adoption and rejection: You seek to cultivate some seemingly solid things and to reject others. Even so, when you are instructed to have no attachment to adoption and rejection, this does not mean that you should ignore karma. In terms of relative truth, even if you have no attachment to adoption and rejection, due to interdependence good and bad actions will still naturally have their corresponding results. Therefore, while abandoning attachment to adoption and rejection, you shouldn't ignore the law of karma. This is called *eliminating misconceptions concerning objects*.

Next is *eliminating misconceptions concerning time*. We all tend to think in terms of the past, the present, and the future. Relatively speaking, past, present, and future exist. Ultimately, however, there is no past, present, or future. The past does not exist now; that past is gone. We may talk of the future, but there is no future; the future doesn't exist. One could say that there is a tiny bit of present, but it's uncertain whether it is actually past or future. Thus, past, present, and future have no real existence. Nevertheless, we talk about the past; we talk about what happened a thousand or two thousand years ago. But that is really just a mental fabrication: There is no thousand or two thousand years ago.

In the same way, directions such as south, west, north, and east also only exist relatively. We can think of north, south, east, and west, but they too are mental fabrications that have no real existence. In his teachings on emptiness the Buddha taught "the emptiness of the vast." In this teaching the Buddha was referring to times and directions, as both time and direction are vast. In spite of being vast, they are empty. They have no reality. Consider the directions. We think of China and Japan as being in the east and California as being in the west. But if you go west from California, you will reach China or Japan. This shows that directions don't have any inherent reality. They are merely conceptual fabrications.

We should avoid attachment to time. In the true nature of the mind there is no time; there is no reality to past, present, or future. The nature of the mind is timeless, so we should eliminate the misconception of being attached to time and direction as real.

The next instruction concerns *eliminating misconceptions concerning essence*. As ordinary beings, when we think of our mind, we think that it's bad, that it is full of defilements and negative thoughts. We think, "I must get rid of this bad mind and obtain the good buddha wisdom." In fact, there isn't really any difference between them. The only thing we need to eliminate is our not recognizing the nature of the mind, and the only thing we need to obtain is the recognition of the nature of the mind. One shouldn't think of the mind as being bad, because the very wisdom we seek is in the mind, and if one can recognize the nature of the mind, then thoughts and even defilements will not be harmful. Lama Shang said, "Fire is something you get from firewood." According to those instructions, in order to obtain the positive, you need the negative. If you have mud, you can grow lotuses. In order to have a good harvest, you need compost. Similarly, by recognizing the nature of the kleshas, one attains wisdom.

The fourth topic of instruction is *eliminating misconceptions concerning nature*. In general, "nature" and "essence" mean nearly the same thing. In this detailed analysis, however, these terms are presented as slightly different in meaning. We generally think of our present mind as inferior and of wisdom as being superior. Here, this misconception concerns the practice of meditation on the nature of the mind. The misconception, therefore, is to think that you are meditating on something superior to the nature of your own mind rather than on the nature of your own mind itself.

When one meditates on the true nature of the mind, nothing is separate from that. Meditating on the nature of the mind means that one is meditating on emptiness, on the *dharmadhatu*, and so on; these are not separate from the mind's nature. In this particular misconception, one thinks of the nature of the mind as something separate from emptiness, something separate from the true nature of phenomena. One sees one's own mind as ordinary or inferior and the nature that one wishes to realize as something different from it. One thinks that one is meditating with an ordinary, inferior mind in order to make it into something better. In fact, one is meditating on nothing other than the nature of the mind itself, which is also the true nature of phenomena. In creation stage meditation, one visualizes oneself as the deity and thinks, "I am the deity," while being aware of the meaning of the visualization.[1] For example, Avalokiteshvara has four arms that represent the four immeasurables and the four activities; his one face represents the single nature of phenomena, and so on. In creation stage meditation, one generates a certainty that one is the deity with these qualities.[2] When one is not engaged in deity practice, one may see oneself as practicing with an ordinary mind and will think that one needs to realize something superior and different. This is a misconception that needs to be eliminated.

You might think that buddhahood is something beyond or even contrary to your own mind, but you must realize that buddhahood is the very nature of the mind itself. The nature of mind is empty, and you should realize that there is nothing to be realized other than this empty nature of the mind. Not knowing this, we think that buddhahood is something higher, something far off. A famous quote states, "There is no Buddha outside of this precious mind." Buddhahood is within the mind itself and cannot be found anywhere else.

The *Sambhuti Tantra* states that buddhahood resides in one's own body. As we have seen, the body is not separate from the mind. But some people think that buddhahood is not within their mind (or within their body) but far away in some other place. In actuality, the Buddha is not in any other place, but because of ignorance and obscuration one seeks the Buddha elsewhere. Trying to find buddhahood someplace other than in the nature of your mind is a misconception.

Saraha said, "I pay homage to the wish-fulfilling jewel of the mind." In the Hinayana and in the sutra tradition of the Mahayana, homage is paid to the Three Jewels, but Saraha pays homage to the mind. He is not paying homage to the mind because it has defilements, which are the causes of karma and samsaric wandering. If one is deluded and has no understanding of the mind, one is in samsara. But if one realizes the true nature of the mind, then there is the ultimate attainment of buddhahood. This is why Saraha pays homage to the wish-fulfilling jewel of the mind. This understanding eliminates misconceptions about the nature of the mind.

The fifth part of this first instruction concerns *eliminating misconceptions about wisdom*. Ultimate wisdom arises through seeing the nature of the mind. One does not attain wisdom through hearing, contemplating, examining, analyzing, having general understanding, having a sharp mind, being good at teaching, or being a scholar. To obtain wisdom, one needs to receive meditation instructions and have the diligence to practice them. Merely having heard some teachings and contemplated them or being learned or having great intelligence will not bring wisdom. Wisdom will come only through meditation, through diligence.

There is a difference between the wisdom gained through hearing and contemplating the teachings and the wisdom that comes from meditation. One can gain a kind of wisdom through hearing the teachings and contemplating them, and through that kind of analysis one can gain a conceptual understanding of emptiness. But this is different from the wisdom of emptiness that comes from directly seeing the nature of the mind. One can conceive of emptiness as being a certain way, but emptiness itself is not really the same. Therefore, a conceptual understanding gained through learning and contemplation can be quite different from the wisdom of direct experience of meditation. The wisdom that comes from learning and contemplation can even be a hindrance to the attainment of wisdom that directly sees the true nature. Therefore, it says in one of the sutras, "The teachings of the true Buddha are not accomplished simply through listening." Just hearing and contemplating the Buddha's teachings will not bring about the attainment of the goal, which can come only from the actual practice of meditation. Merely having the wisdom that comes from learning and contemplation is like being swept downstream by a river but not drinking the water and then dying of thirst. Similarly, in receiving the Buddhist teachings, one may gain a conceptual understanding through listening and contemplation, but one will not attain the goal, which is the wisdom that comes from meditation.

These misconceptions are not errors that one makes in meditation. They are slight errors in understanding that can cause obstacles to one's meditation. These errors prevent one's meditation from occurring or developing. For this reason, this teaching is given on enhancing the result of meditation through eliminating the five misconceptions.

DEVELOPING THE THREE SKILLS

The next topic is enhancing the result through the instructions on the three skills. The first of these is *skill at commencing meditation*. If the mind is in stillness, meditate on that stillness; if the mind is in movement, meditate on that movement; if a defilement arises, meditate on that defilement; and if happiness or unhappiness arises, meditate on that. Whatever arises, meditate upon it and recognize its nature as emptiness and clarity. *An Ocean of the Ultimate Meaning* gives several quotations: "Like the weaving of a Brahmin's thread, the yogin's awareness should be relaxed." Thus, the mind should be relaxed and not too tight. And, "Like a candle flame that is not disturbed by the wind, the mind should be clear and without the distraction of thought."

There is another quote: "Just as the stars and planets appear as reflections in the sea, so do all appearances and all that exists rest within Mahamudra." The planets, stars, sun, and moon all appear distinctly and clearly on the surface of the ocean. They are not within the ocean itself, but their images appear there. Similarly, whatever appears, whether the mind is in stillness or in movement, does not transcend Mahamudra. Another quote says, "Like the constant flow of a river, the mind continually rests in the dharmakaya." The mind continuously, at all times, has this true nature, which is the true nature of phenomena, and in meditation the mind is always resting in that.

While in meditation, one simply rests in the nature of mind exactly as it is. One shouldn't think that this meditation needs something profound and impressive, some extreme emptiness or especially strong clarity. That would be a contrived, artificially created meditation. Skill in the commencement of meditation means having a meditation that is relaxed and uncontrived, in which one rests in the nature of the mind just as it is. That is the first skill.

The second skill is *preventing any loss of meditation*. Your meditation practice should be very clear and pure, and in order to achieve this, rather than meditating for long periods, you should do a number of clear, short meditation sessions. If you try to do this meditation for a long period, you are likely to become unaware of the presence of thoughts. Your meditation should have clarity and be very sharp. Here "clarity" means being free from any kind of dullness. "Sharp" means that you aspire to and delight in the meditation, so that you aren't forcing yourself and it isn't difficult. The way to maintain a pure, clear meditation is to begin with clarity and sharpness and then to continue the meditation only for as long as you can maintain that quality. Apply this instruction to the different meditations: when the mind is still, when it is in movement, when a defilement arises, and so on. As a result, your meditation will progress.

The third instruction concerns *nurturing experience without attachment*. In the practice of meditation, all kinds of experiences may arise, but one should not have any attachment to them. What kinds of experiences arise in meditation? They can be grouped into three kinds: experiences of bliss, clarity, and nonthought. Whatever arises, don't have any attachment to it. If bliss, clarity, or nonthought arises, don't think, "Oh, this is something very good." If you have attachment, then pride and envy can also develop, so you shouldn't engage in good, bad, or neutral thoughts about these experiences. If you can see these experiences as insignificant and have no attachment to them, your practice will eventually give rise to realization. Realization comes as a result of avoiding attachment to experiences in meditation.

Becoming attached is called "losing realization for the sake of experience." For example, you might have an experience of bliss and think, "This is really good; this is what I need." Consequently, you develop an attachment to it. You might react in the same way to an experience of clarity or nonthought and make obtaining that experience the most important thing in your meditation. By doing this, you lose realization. One needs to have experiences in meditation, but becoming attached to them is a fault, so you need to be skilled in nurturing experience without any attachment.

What is meant by experience and realization? What is the difference between them? It is said that experience is something that is not beyond concepts, so that one may think, "This is excellent," and then develop attachment. The experiences of bliss and so on can be very strong, so that one thinks, "This is really excellent, wonderful, and pleasant," and wishes for more such experiences. But whether one's experiences are strong or weak, one should be without attachment to them.

In *The Ocean of Songs of the Kagyu Lineage* (published as *The Rain of Wisdom*), there is a description of how Gampopa met Milarepa and then practiced and had all kinds of experiences. Once he had a vision of the mandala of Red Hevajra. Another time he had a vision of the mandala of White Chakrasamvara. Gampopa thought, "It must be excellent to have a vision of the yidam deities," and he told Milarepa about his experiences. Milarepa replied, "It's not good, it's not bad,

it's not a fault, it's not a quality. What you need to do is meditate."
One time for Gampopa everything went black; another time he saw
all the hells; and once the whole world was spinning until he vom-
ited. He thought he was doing something wrong in his meditation,
so again he went to Milarepa. Milarepa said, "There is nothing
wrong, there is nothing right. It isn't a fault, it isn't a quality. Just
carry on with meditation."

Milarepa said that this was like a person squeezing his eyes. If you
squeeze your eyes, you can see two moons, and you might think,
"This is really wonderful—I can see two moons. This means I'm
very special, as everyone else can see only one." Someone else doing
the same thing might get frightened and think, "What's wrong with
me? Everybody else sees one moon, but I see two. Something terrible is happening to me." In fact, nothing special or terrible is happening at all; these two people are just squeezing their eyes. It is the same
with meditation experiences: They aren't really a positive quality,
and they aren't really a fault. Rather than feeling proud or frightened
about meditation experiences, one needs to see the true nature of the
mind. This will free one from any error or mistake.

Some people have all kinds of different experiences—visual experiences of places or colors, and experiences of sensations. But if you
become attached to any of them, you will hope that they come again,
and if they don't reoccur, you will seek them out, and in this way
your meditation will become contrived. Some people may be frightened by the experiences they have in meditation and become afraid
to meditate. But all these experiences are just creations of the mind,
so there is no reason for fear, pride, happiness, or attachment. Avoid
attachment to whatever experiences arise, and instead just meditate
on the nature of the mind. If you can focus on the nature of the
mind, then you will gain realization.

One type of experience is physical or mental bliss. Sometimes
the body is filled with bliss. Attachment to that bliss can lead to depression and loss of interest in meditation when the bliss does not

reoccur. Whatever experiences of bliss or sadness arise in one's meditation, one should not develop attachment.

The experience of clarity means seeing various forms—shapes, colors, disks of light, and so on—or just a state of clarity in the mind. This experience comes and goes. An experience of nonthought can also occur, in which thoughts just naturally cease. Sometimes no thoughts are arising, and at other times many thoughts arise. Avoid attachment to these experiences, because they are transitory. Instead of desiring these experiences, think, "In my meditation I am looking at the nature of the mind, so I'm not going to develop attachment to any experiences." Without attachment or aversion to high or low experiences, continue looking at the nature of the mind. That is how to be skilled in nurturing experiences without attachment.

AVOIDING THE FOUR DEVIATIONS

The next set of instructions on enhancing the result concerns four possible deviations in meditation. A deviation is like going down a wrong road, so that one doesn't arrive at the direct experience of meditation but arrives instead at a conceptual understanding, which is then mistaken for the experience of meditation.

The first deviation concerns *the nature of knowledge*, in which emptiness becomes an object of knowledge. One can use various kinds of reasoning to establish the emptiness of phenomena. One can look at how phenomena arise; one can look at the entity itself; one can look at how phenomena are dependent upon each other; and so on. Thus, one gains some certainty in understanding that the nature of external phenomena is emptiness. With a conceptual understanding, one may think of emptiness as nonexistence. Conceptual understanding is relative, so that if it is said that things have no existence, then nonexistence is generally conceived of as a "thing." When hearing that phenomena have no real existence, one might immediately think, "That must mean that they are nonexistent." When hearing that phenomena are not nonexistent, then one might think, "Well, then they must be existent." If the text speaks of the union of existence and nonexistence, then one might think of this as being like a white thread and a black thread joined together. This is because of a relative, conceptual understanding.

Shantideva taught that the nature of emptiness is beyond conceptual understanding. The instructions of the great siddhas come from their direct experience of the nature of mind. Therefore, their understanding of "it is not existent, it is not nonexistent" is not a conceptual, relative understanding.

From the perspective of a relative, conceptual understanding, one will think that something has to be eliminated, that one has to get rid of reality in order to experience emptiness. Again, this makes the realization of emptiness something far off and difficult to attain. If instead one meditates directly on the nature of the mind, the realization of emptiness is easier to achieve. Although the reasoning that establishes the emptiness of phenomena is in itself good, it is difficult to attain realization by using this approach. It is best to use both approaches. If you gain some realization in meditation, then that realization will help to increase your conceptual understanding derived through reasoning. And your analytical understanding will help the realization that comes from meditation.

The second deviation is *sealing with emptiness*. For example, if you do a good action, it is sealed with emptiness, or purified of the triplism of subject, object, and action or instrument of the action. If you perform an act of generosity, seal it with emptiness by recollecting that the giver, the given, and the recipient of the giving are all devoid of any real nature. This is called sealing the action with emptiness. If you are doing the practice of deity visualization, you recite the mantra OM SVABHAVA SHUDDHA SARVA DHARMA SVABHAVA SHUDDHO HAM, which means that everything becomes emptiness and from emptiness things arise; in this way, you seal the practice with emptiness.

It is beneficial to apply the seal of emptiness, but if in this meditation you think solely in terms of sealing with emptiness, this is not beneficial. For some, sealing with emptiness is just a matter of words; one just thinks, "Everything has become empty." Or one may think of emptiness as being nothingness. In this meditation, instead of sealing it with emptiness, look directly at the empty nature of the mind itself; you will see that it is not just emptiness alone, and you will have a genuine experience of the empty nature. Therefore, although sealing with emptiness is in itself beneficial, it is not enough. If you practice meditation purely in terms of sealing with emptiness, your meditation will have fallen into that deviation.

The third deviation is *emptiness as a remedy*. One normally thinks of a klesha, a bad thought, as an existent thing and a remedy as something that will overcome it. But that is not what one should be doing in this meditation; practicing in that way would be the deviation of emptiness as a remedy. In this meditation, one should look at the very nature of the defilement that arises in order to see its primordial essence. Whatever klesha arises—anger, attachment, and so on—look at its essence to see where it arises from, where it is, where it disappears to. If you see its essence, that klesha will be self-liberated, and there will be no need to apply any other remedy to it. This is what we should be doing in this meditation. If instead you apply emptiness as a remedy against a defilement, then you have the defilement as one thing and emptiness-as-remedy as another thing and they're set to fight each other until emptiness can bring the defilement to an end. Generally speaking, there's nothing wrong in doing that, but it's not appropriate in the context of this meditation, where one should see the very essence of the defilement as emptiness. If instead you use emptiness as a remedy against the defilement, that is the deviation of emptiness as a remedy.

The fourth deviation is *taking emptiness as the path*. Generally speaking, the nature of the mind is something that we have not looked at and do not know. Therefore, we need to look at the nature of the mind and be able to see it, to know it. But is it sufficient merely to have seen the nature of the mind? No, it is not, because of the strength of our habituation. We have to look again and again in order to familiarize ourselves with seeing the mind's true nature. That is why we practice meditation. We meditate on the nature of the mind, and that is the path. But if we think, "I am doing this meditation to gain the result of the path," although, generally speaking, that is the right view, it's not correct in the context of this meditation practice. Here this approach becomes the deviation of mistakenly taking emptiness as the path.

In addition to the four kinds of deviations, there are seventeen ways of going astray. *An Ocean of the Ultimate Meaning* gives the practitioner remedies for each of these errors, in case any of them occurs. It's very possible that your meditation will go well and none of these seventeen errors will occur, or perhaps only one or two will occur, but all the remedies are taught.

(1) If one has experiences in meditation—experiences of bliss, clarity, or nonthought, for example—one should identify what specific type of experience one is having. (2) If it is an experience of bliss, determine whether the experience is of defiled bliss or immaculate bliss. If one develops an attachment to the experience of bliss, one will stray into the realm of desire, which means that one will take rebirth in the desire realm, within which there are many levels of existence. One will not be reborn in any of the lower existences but will take rebirth in one of the higher existences of the desire realm.

(3) If an experience of clarity arises, one should not have attachment to it. If one develops attachment to clarity, the result will be rebirth in the form realms. (4) If one develops attachment to the experience of nonthought, it will lead to rebirth in the formless realm. Within the formless realm there are four different states; one is reborn there through the power of meditation, so these states have the characteristics of states of meditation. In the formless realm, there is no form, but there are qualities.

(5) If one has strong attachment to a nonconceptual state, to a state of equanimity, then one will be reborn in the formless level

known as Infinite Space. (6) If one has attachment to a state of non-thought and thinks of it as being just mind, one will be reborn in the state called Infinite Consciousness. (7) If one has attachment to a state of nonthought that one perceives as being just nothing, then one will be reborn in the state called Nothing Whatsoever. (8) And if one has a powerful state of nonthought with attachment, then one will be reborn in the state called Neither Existent nor Nonexistent.

(9) When these experiences arise and you can taste them strongly, be careful not to develop attachment to them. Instead, look into the essence of whatever experience arises. Whatever experiences come—bliss, clarity, or equanimity—don't try to develop them or get rid of them; just recognize their essence, and no harm will come from having these experiences. Otherwise, one can go astray into rebirth in the four states of the formless realm. The remedy is merely to look into the experiences in the same way that one looks into one's own face.

(10) Next is the fault of the absence of compassion. If one is lacking compassion, one may stray into the Hinayana, the lower path. While in itself this lower yana is something good, it is not able to bring one to the full result. So one needs to have compassion.

(11) The method aspect enhances the result of wisdom, while simultaneously wisdom enhances the results gained from the method. If one performs good actions and seals them with emptiness in a way that is free from a belief in the reality of the three aspects of an action, then wisdom will enhance this practice of good actions, which is the method side. But the practice of method also enhances the wisdom, so that one doesn't solely practice meditation but also performs good actions that accumulate merit. One does the practice of meditation on deities, but by accompanying this with good actions, one enhances wisdom. In these tenth and eleventh points, method enhances wisdom and wisdom enhances method.

(12) The wisdom of emptiness by itself is not enough; it needs to be accompanied by compassion. (13) Compassion by itself is not enough; it needs to be accompanied by the wisdom of vipashyana.

(14) Shamatha by itself without vipashyana would not be benefi-cial; shamatha needs to be accompanied by insight meditation. (15) Vipashyana alone is not sufficient: Vipashyana cannot develop if it is not accompanied by shamatha.

Thus, we see that compassion without emptiness and emptiness without compassion are incomplete, so one should develop a union of compassion and emptiness. Similarly, method without wisdom and wisdom without method are also not right. One needs to have method and wisdom together. As well, shamatha without vipashyana and vipashyana without shamatha are not right. One needs to have the union of both.

(16) Generally, one's conduct should not be ordinary. One should have mindfulness, awareness, and attentiveness and should practice good actions. Doing this will enhance the result of meditation. (17) Kleshas, suffering, and obstacles may arise. Whether you are ex-periencing a happy or a sad event, try to see the nature of that experi-ence without viewing it as a fault or a quality. If you can simply see the empty essence of the experience, it will cease to be harmful. At the beginning, this may be difficult to do, but with diligence in meditation, you will gradually improve. You will be able to see the empty nature of these difficult circumstances so that they become harmless.

These are the seventeen ways one might go astray. It is not defi-nite that these seventeen errors will occur, but if any of them do happen, you will be able to recognize them.

PASSING THROUGH THE THREE DANGEROUS PATHWAYS

The next teaching on the enhancement of the result is the instruction on passing through the three dangerous pathways. These are faults that can arise, like enemies appearing. Although these faults are possi-ble, if one has love and compassion, faith and devotion, and good meditation, it is unlikely that they will arise. If they don't occur, one just carries on naturally. If they do, one needs to recognize and eliminate them.

The first fault is *emptiness arising as an enemy*. This is not something that occurs during meditation but is the result of a conceptual idea of emptiness. If it occurs, it is serious and dangerous. However, if one has love and compassion, faith and devotion, and good meditation, it will not occur. If it does happen, it needs to be recognized and removed.

Emptiness arising as an enemy means that one has developed attachment to emptiness. Consequently, one thinks that the accumulation of good and bad actions is just empty and that no real result comes from the accumulation of karma. Believing that there is no particular reason to cultivate positive actions or eliminate negative actions, one will not eliminate bad actions or cultivate good actions. In this way, emptiness has become an enemy. As a result, one wanders into darkness, which means that one sinks into a bad state. Normally, to recognize emptiness as emptiness is a very good thing, but in this case it becomes a fault. This is not something that generally happens to meditators, but it is a possible fault that should be recognized and avoided.

Sometimes Mahamudra and Dzogchen instructions are kept secret. These instructions are beneficial to anyone who puts them into practice, but they are sometimes kept secret in order to avoid the possibility that emptiness might arise as an enemy for some individuals. Someone might receive this teaching and, generating only a conceptual understanding of it rather than gaining experience and realization in meditation, might develop attachment to emptiness and consequently dismiss the idea of being attentive to the results of one's actions. It is to avoid that danger that the Mahamudra and Dzogchen instructions are kept secret.

In *An Ocean of the Ultimate Meaning*, Wangchuk Dorje shows that this is not only his view. In the sutra tradition, this is also taught by Nagarjuna in the text *Mulaprajña* (*The Root Wisdom of the Middle*

Way). Nagarjuna says that if you can realize emptiness, this is excellent, but there is also the danger that you may misunderstand it. Those with great wisdom will be able to understand emptiness, but those with little wisdom will misunderstand it and be ruined, which means they will be harmed by their misconception of emptiness. Nagarjuna compares this to grasping a snake in order to obtain a medicinal substance from it. Someone who knows how to seize a poisonous snake will be able to obtain the medicine, but someone who doesn't know how may be bitten and poisoned. In the same way, one might misunderstand emptiness so that emptiness becomes harmful to oneself.

Nagarjuna said, "Those who are wise should understand emptiness and through meditation on it gain realization of emptiness." That is what one should do to understand emptiness: Meditate on it and realize it. One should not merely have a simplistic understanding of emptiness, develop attachment to emptiness, or cling to the idea of emptiness. This is like wandering into darkness. To be free of this fault, first one should understand that the nature of phenomena is emptiness: Phenomena are empty of any real nature of their own. Then, by looking at the mind, one sees that the mind is empty of any real nature. In this way one will, in the end, gain experience and realization and know the true nature of phenomena and the mind.

In spite of our seeing this empty nature, appearances still arise unceasingly. In the sutra tradition, both ultimate and relative truth are taught. In terms of ultimate truth, the nature of phenomena has no reality. It is empty. In terms of relative truth, phenomena are interdependent, and interdependence is the unceasing arising of phenomena. The arising of appearances is said to have no reality. In this sense, it is sometimes described as an illusion or a mirage; but at the same time, phenomena are not like a mirage or an illusion, which have no essence at all. There is still interdependence, the infallibility of relative phenomena. For example, if you touch fire, you will be burned; fire has the quality of burning. If you touch water, you get wet; water has the quality of wetness. Similarly, if you do a good action, the result will be happiness; if you do a bad action, the result will be suffering. In terms of relative phenomena, causes ripen into results. A cause will definitely bring a result, and a result will come from a cause. This is the infallible interdependence of phenomena.

The Mahamudra instructions speak of the empty nature of the mind, of emptiness and clarity. As described in *An Ocean of the Ultimate Meaning*, there is also the unceasing power of the complete arising of appearances. The unceasing power, the luminosity of appearances, means that there is cause and result—there are good and bad actions, and there is interdependence. Although appearances ultimately have no reality, as a result of interdependence they appear as if they actually exist. Therefore, if there is a cause, there will certainly be a result. This is the infallibility of relative phenomena.

By understanding emptiness, one gains a realization that is like space. But, at the same time, one should unite this realization with very fine conduct. This means that with regard to one's behavior one knows that even the smallest good or bad action is important. One is attentive to the finest details of one's motivation and conduct and the development of love, compassion, faith, and devotion. These are not ignored or considered unimportant. In this way, one can unite fine conduct with realization, which means that realization does not conflict with conduct and conduct does not conflict with realization. Instead, interdependence becomes the gathering of excellent qualities; one is able to accumulate good conduct together with realization. One does not ignore meditation and realization and concentrate on the details of conduct. Nor does one cultivate some kind of externally oriented meditation with a simplistic view of emptiness and consider the details of one's conduct unimportant. Instead, there is the union of conduct and realization. One's conduct does not diminish realization, and realization does not diminish conduct.

But then someone might ask, "Isn't it taught that we should have no adoption or rejection?" That is true; it is taught that we should not have attachment to that which is to be eliminated or to the remedy. So we need to avoid becoming attached to what needs to be eliminated as well as to the idea that the remedy itself is real. Although the nature of the mind is emptiness, there is an unceasing clarity. With regard to the clarity aspect, there is an unending arising of phenomena as interdependent origination. This interdependence is infallible. Thus, although phenomena are ultimately devoid of any reality, as a result of their infallible interdependence, one does not ignore the law of cause and result.

We are taught, on the one hand, to avoid attachment to adoption or rejection and, on the other hand, that one must not have a simplistic understanding of emptiness and ignore the law of karma. Both of these teachings are important. The error of emptiness becoming one's enemy does not usually occur, but if it did, it would be very dangerous. For that reason, this teaching is given.

The second possible enemy is *compassion arising as an enemy*. Generally, compassion is something that we strive to develop; we need to develop compassion toward beings who are suffering and beings who are not suffering. We wish all beings to be free from suffering. Although compassion is generally something that we need to develop, it is possible to develop mistaken compassion.

Someone might think, "What I really have to do is benefit beings and free them from suffering. Just working for my own benefit alone is not going to bring me to buddhahood, so I should apply myself to helping others." This is just a conceptual understanding. Such a person may then abandon good meditation and engage in ordinary worldly activities to help other beings, leaving behind any development of experience and realization. Doing this comes from the wish to benefit beings, but the result is that one can benefit them only in temporary ways; one cannot bring them lasting benefit. In this way, compassion can become one's enemy.

It is good to develop compassion, but one should also continue with one's practice. In that way, one's meditation will progress and bring experience and realization, which will eventually bring inconceivable benefit to other beings. The main point here is that it is important not to lose one's meditation in the process of developing compassion. To cultivate experience and realization through meditation is very important and is the remedy for compassion becoming one's enemy.

The third enemy is *cause and result arising as an enemy.* Someone who is practicing meditation and studying the meditation instructions may, due to a limited understanding, decide that they need to study more and to postpone their meditation practice. They may think, "In order to realize the true nature of the mind, I need to master all these branches of knowledge, so I will postpone my meditation practice until I've done that." Generally speaking, mastering these different branches of knowledge is very good, but in this case pursuing knowledge in this way is harmful for one's practice of meditation.

For example, I once met a man, quite an old man, who was interested in meditating well. In order to do that, he had decided it was first necessary to study the *Lotus Sutra.* But the *Lotus Sutra* is in Chinese, so first he had to learn Chinese. This is a very long road to take in order to arrive at meditation—first he had to learn Chinese, then study the sutra, and only then begin to meditate. He would have been much better off just starting with meditation. This is an example of cause and result becoming an enemy—by accumulating so many causes to get your result, you put the result farther and farther into the future.

Generally it is good to study, but if studying is harmful to your practice—and therefore harmful to the development of experience and realization—then it becomes an obstacle. It's not that you need to abandon all studying, but if it is harmful to your practice, then cause and result has become an enemy. Studying in such a way that you are still able to maintain your practice is the remedy for cause and result becoming an enemy.

Previously, we examined the four deviations and the seventeen different ways of going astray. The four deviations are more serious than the seventeen ways that we can go astray. This section has been about emptiness, compassion, and cause and result becoming one's enemies. If compassion and cause and result become enemies, this will result in a temporary obstacle to meditation or will prevent meditation from progressing, but these obstacles don't cause great harm. Emptiness becoming an enemy rarely happens, but if it does, it will cause great harm, so we should be very careful that it does not occur. These deviations, strayings, and transformations into enemies are not errors in meditation. They are errors in one's way of thinking. These faults occur because of mistaken motivations or understandings. Therefore, once we recognize these faults, we can easily correct them.

XI

Eliminating Obstacles

In the previous chapter we looked at enhancing the benefit of practice by avoiding deviations and faults, such as emptiness arising as an enemy. When these occur, they hinder practice, and by eliminating them one is able to develop experience and realization. As we have already discussed, if emptiness, compassion, and cause and result become enemies, they should be recognized as such, and the problem is then easily removed. The second aspect of enhancing the results of practice concerns eliminating obstacles. These are stronger and more difficult to remove, as simply recognizing them doesn't work. There are three such obstacles.

THE OBSTACLE OF ILLNESS

The first obstacle is illness. We have obtained a human body, a precious human existence with the eighteen qualities, the freedoms and leisures to practice the Dharma. When we say that our human existence is precious, this means that it is precious as a basis for practicing the Dharma. If the body is healthy and free from illness, we will be able to practice the Dharma free from any obstacle. If we become ill, such an obstacle may prevent us from practicing the Dharma.

This obstacle of illness can be eliminated through meditation. Tibetan medicine has two ways of classifying illness. First, illnesses can be grouped into three types: illnesses of air, bile, and phlegm. Because of air, bile, or phlegm, the five elements of earth, air, fire, water, and space become agitated, and this causes illness. A second classification of illnesses divides them into hot and cold illnesses.

The air element can cause disturbance in the mind and ill health in the body. Air has an agitating effect that causes instability in the mind, so one becomes agitated, disturbed, or depressed. This agitation of the mind also causes agitation in the channels in the body. What is the method for eliminating the obstacle of illness from air? Force or suppression will not solve this problem. The remedy is shamatha meditation, which brings about a natural state of relaxation and stillness. This stillness from shamatha will eliminate the agitation caused by the air element. Eliminating the agitation removes the disturbance in the mind and the ill health that it causes. Therefore, shamatha meditation is the method for eliminating the obstacle of illnesses from air.

On the other hand, vipashyana meditation is the method that will eliminate illnesses from bile and phlegm. Bile and phlegm are stable but unclear; they have the quality of dullness. As a result of the power of bile or phlegm, the movement of airs in the channels of the body may be obstructed, which causes illness. In order to remove this effect of bile and phlegm, one needs clarity and wisdom. Clarity will eliminate the dulling effect of bile and phlegm and the illnesses they cause. In order to develop clarity and wisdom, one practices vipashyana.

The body is composed of the four elements of earth, air, fire, and water. (There is also an expanded list of six elements that includes space and consciousness. These last two are the aspects of emptiness and clarity.) *An Ocean of the Ultimate Meaning* describes how the earth element has the quality of solidity and stability; the quality of water is wetness; the quality of fire is heat; and the quality of air is movement. If all these elements are in balance, then the body's air, phlegm, and bile are in balance, and the body is healthy. If there is an imbalance of one of these—say, a preponderance of phlegm—then there will be a corresponding imbalance in the elements of earth and water. The earth element will become heavy and the water element will sink downward.

One needs a remedy for the dullness and stupor that occur as a result of this imbalance. The remedy is insight meditation. Vipashyana has the quality of clarity, which will counteract dullness and the heaviness of earth and the sinking quality of water caused by the imbalance of phlegm. These imbalances will be eliminated by the clarity of vipashyana.

An imbalance of bile can occur due to an excess of the elements of fire and air. This imbalance causes a rising upward of fire and a violent movement of the air, which causes ill health. To counteract this, one practices shamatha meditation, which will bring down the fire and air. In this way, shamatha acts as a remedy for illnesses caused by the imbalance of the fire and air elements.

In terms of hot and cold illnesses, as shamatha has a cooling effect, it is the remedy for hot illnesses. Vipashyana is beneficial for cold illnesses because it has a quality of light and warmth. So generally speaking, practicing shamatha will benefit a hot illness, and practicing vipashyana will benefit a cold illness.

More specifically, in the context of Mahamudra, if you are sick, look at the nature of that illness or pain. Look to see what it is. You will find that it has no real nature of its own, and seeing this will pacify the experience of illness. If there is pain, even if it is very sharp or strong, look at the nature of that pain to see where it arises from and so on, and you will see that pain is empty of any nature of its own. Then rest in meditation. This doesn't mean that the pain will stop, but the experiences of sickness and pain will be diminished, and as a result, they will be less harmful to the mind and body. This approach of looking at the nature of the sensation of pain is called "eliminating the obstacle of illness," or "adopting pain as the path."

In terms of adopting pain as the path, the great masters and siddhas of the past taught that one can do this even if one is healthy. Pinch yourself, and you will feel pain, an undesirable sensation. Look at the nature of that pain. Looking at its nature will not make the pain itself vanish, but if you see its empty nature, the pain becomes harmless to your mind. You can begin this practice of adopting pain as the path by training with such small pains. By habituating yourself in this way, you will be able to progress to adopting illness and pain as the path.

THE OBSTACLE OF DEMONS

Next is the elimination of the obstacle of demons. There are two descriptions of demons. Some say that demons are beings. Others say that there are no such beings as demons and that what happens is the result of one's actions in this life and past lives. One's actions in the past can create a karmic debt. If you have done something harmful to another in the past, you will eventually experience a similar harmful action done to you. For example, if you have stolen from someone, eventually you will have the experience of being stolen from. It's as if you've borrowed something that has to be repaid.

The obstacle of illness primarily concerns the body and physical discomfort. The obstacle of demons arises primarily in the mind. Sometimes you may feel great fear, sadness, regret, or other strong emotion. You may think that these emotions are caused by some being, by a demon, because there is no reason to be disturbed and yet you are experiencing great mental suffering. This is what is meant by the obstacle of demons.

This is an obstacle to the practice of meditation and should be eliminated. Shamatha makes the mind still and calm, and vipashyana looks at the nature of depression or sadness to see its empty nature. Sometimes vipashyana can eliminate the obstacle. At other times it cannot, but by continuing to apply vipashyana one becomes adept, and eventually such obstacles will be easily overcome.

If you can use vipashyana to eliminate obstacles or hindrances, then you should do so. But some people have a great deal of fear and unhappiness and are so disturbed that they are unable to practice

vipashyana. In these circumstances, such persons should practice shamatha. Through shamatha practice, the mind will become more
calm, and when the fear and agitation have been calmed, the person
will then be able to practice vipashyana. In that way, the obstacle can
be eliminated.

There is also the teaching of adopting suffering as the path. This
instruction applies not only to suffering that is the result of unex-
plained mental states (that is, demons) but also to suffering that is the
result of any bad circumstances that one encounters. When things go
badly, there is unhappiness and suffering, but these can be adopted as
the path. When present circumstances cause worry or unhappiness,
instead of seeing this suffering as something real, use the practice of
vipashyana to look at its nature. This allows the mind to become
more relaxed and open in the midst of difficult circumstances. This
is adopting suffering as the path.

THE OBSTACLES TO MEDITATION

The third class of obstacles consists of obstacles to meditation. There
are many such obstacles—maliciousness, doubt, regret, and so on—
but they can be condensed into two categories: agitation and dullness. These two obstacles include all others, so that agitation includes
maliciousness, doubt, regret, and so on. Dullness is when the mind is
stuporous and unclear.

There are a variety of remedies to these obstacles. As we saw
earlier, for dullness, one can think of the qualities of the Buddha,
contemplate the problems of samsara, make physical adjustments, do
visualizations, and so on. Here, the specific method of removing
dullness through guru yoga is taught. When the mind becomes unclear, dull, and drowsy, imagine that above your head is Amitabha,
one of the five family buddhas, red in color, who is in essence your
guru. All the buddhas, bodhisattvas, and gurus of the lineage merge
into him. Out of your faith and devotion and supplication to him,
bright red light rays emanate from his body and fill your own body,

eliminating the four kinds of dullness. The many kinds of dullness can be summarized into four: dullness due to time,[1] dullness due to physical conduct, dullness due to contamination, and dullness due to the ripening of karma. All four of these types of dullness are eliminated by the bright red light that fills your entire body. Then your body transforms into a sphere of white light that is as bright as the sun or moon, so that it illuminates all the pure realms. The light gradually vanishes, and you rest in a state of knowing that is very clear and sharp. This is a method for eliminating dullness of mind.

As a remedy for agitation, when many thoughts are arising, imagine the guru in the form of Vajrasattva in your heart on a four-petaled lotus. Vajrasattva, who is blue in color, is in the center as Akshobhya Buddha. On the four petals are the four buddhas Vairochana, Ratnasambhava, Amitabha, and Amoghasiddhi. All the buddhas are blue in color, and they are surrounded by dakas, dakinis, buddhas, and bodhisattvas. From this encircling entourage, blue light rays radiate to the guru in the form of Vajrasattva and encircle him like a network of light. This visualization diminishes agitation.

Another method, which has been taught in other texts, is adopting the bardo as the path. When we are alive, we have what is called an illusory body of flesh and blood. This body is an appearance of the mind. Although at death this appearance ceases, after death one still has the appearance of a body. It's the same when we dream. The mind has sunk into sleep, and the appearance of the body ceases, but in the dream one has a body, which is an appearance from the mind. Just as one has the appearance of a body in dreams, after death we also have the appearance of a body.

Within the body there are the channels, airs, and bindus located in the chakras. We can visualize these bindus as peaceful and wrathful deities. At death this naturally present body expands outward and takes on the appearance of the peaceful and wrathful deities. If one has previously meditated and recognized the nature of appearances, one will see that these bardo appearances are no different from the appearances in one's previous meditation practice. One will recognize the first bardo of the true nature of phenomena. But if one has no meditation training, one will not recognize what is occurring and will lose consciousness. Then when one revives, one will see the bardo of the *sambhogakaya*, in which there is the appearance of the peaceful and wrathful deities. These peaceful and wrathful deities appear naturally; they are not created by meditation. They appear because they are naturally present within the key points of the body. It is the same as in the Dzogchen tradition's practice of *tögal*. Similarly, in the Kagyu tradition there is the practice of the completion stage of Kalachakra, in which there is meditation in darkness and meditation on the light of the sun. At that time what are called empty forms appear. These empty forms, which are lights and so on, are not being caused to appear but are naturally present in key places in the body. So in the bardo the peaceful and wrathful deities appear naturally. Those who are trained in the Dharma will be able to recognize the nature of these appearances within meditation. For those who haven't trained in the Dharma, it's important that they not be overcome by fear but have stability of mind so that they can recognize what is occurring.

There is a simple way to begin this practice of adopting the bardo as the path. First close your eyes very tightly. At first there is just darkness, so you don't see anything. Then after a while, lights, colors, and shapes will start to appear and will become stronger and stronger until they are very bright and luminous. At this time, you should have a relaxed mind: Rest in the state of meditation, and look into the nature of these appearances. Rest in this meditation exactly as you do after looking at the mind in stillness or looking at the mind in movement. In that way, the lights will cease to be so intense and bright. This is a method for eliminating the fear that can arise in the bardo.

If you clench your teeth tightly together, you will hear a sound in your ears. These are naturally arising sounds, not sounds that come from outside. This sound becomes louder and louder, but just relax, look at its nature, and rest in that meditation. The sound will then diminish. That is an easy way to practice adopting the bardo as the path.

XII

Proceeding along the Path

The Four Yogas of Mahamudra

We have been learning about the nature of the mind: seeing how it is in a state of delusion and how it is when its true nature is seen. When the mind is in a state of delusion, it is in the form of the eight consciousnesses. When we see the mind's true nature, the mind manifests as the five wisdoms.[1]

The Sanskrit word *jñana* means wisdom or knowledge. In Tibetan the term is *yeshe*. *She* means knowledge, but when *jñana* was translated into Tibetan, the extra syllable *ye* was added. *Yeshe* means wisdom that is above and beyond common knowledge—the *ye* syllable indicates knowledge of the true nature of the mind. However, this knowledge is not something that is newly created. It has always been primordially present. The word for consciousness in Sanskrit is *vijñana*, which in Tibetan is *namshe*. The meaning is the same. *She* again means knowledge, and *nam* means that there is clarity, a very clear knowing; this is what is meant by consciousness. When the mind ceases to be deluded, it is not that we have eliminated consciousness, this clear knowing. It is not that delusion occurs because this state of clear knowing has become dull or darkened. Delusion is not a state of darkness but a state of clarity—the clarity of consciousness. There is clear perception of form, sound, smell, and so on. There's a vivid perception of form, self, "I," and reality. So it's through the clarity of these things that one is in a state of delusion. This vivid knowledge is grouped into eight kinds, the eight consciousnesses.

We speak of clarity in shamatha and clarity in vipashyana, but these are two different kinds of clarity. When we talk of clarity in shamatha, it means that the sixth consciousness has become peaceful and stable, yet there is no cessation of the clarity of the mind. There is the ongoing presence of the clarity of the eighth consciousness. But in vipashyana meditation, there is a direct perception. In all, there are four kinds of direct perceptions. First, there is the *direct perception of the sensory consciousnesses.* Second, there is the *direct perception of the mental consciousness.* This mental consciousness can be either conceptual or nonconceptual.[2] The aspect of the mental consciousness that follows the sensory consciousness is the nonconceptual aspect. The third kind is the *direct perception of self-knowing.* This is the fact that the mind is not concealed from itself. The fourth kind of direct perception is called the *direct perception of the yogin.*

What is meant by the direct perception of the yogin? There are two kinds of yogic direct perception. Through the power of meditation one can develop clairvoyance, the direct perception of what is in the minds of others and the ability to see all kinds of things. That is one kind of direct perception of the yogin, but this, together with all the other types of direct perception, belongs to the category of relative phenomena. Clairvoyance, the sensory consciousnesses, the mental consciousness, and self-knowing are all externally directed toward relative phenomena. Then there is the second kind of direct perception of the yogin, which can be described as the sixth consciousness turned inward upon itself, or alternatively as the eighth consciousness looking at the mental consciousness. In either case, this is nonconceptual direct perception. This is the direct perception of true nature within vipashyana meditation.

When the consciousnesses are externally directed, they appear to be different, distinct consciousnesses: the consciousness of the eye, the nose, and so on, and the sixth mental consciousness. But when we turn the mind inward, all these consciousnesses become the same, and no distinction can be made between them. It is as if there is only one consciousness in that one cannot find or identify any individual, distinct consciousnesses. This is the direct perception of the sixth consciousness turned inward. This direct perception is nonconceptual, so it is not through the medium of the conceptual sixth consciousness. Rather, this is the direct perception of self-knowing wisdom. It is the mind seeing its own nature. This is how we use our consciousnesses in the vipashyana of Mahamudra.

In the practice of Mahamudra meditation, one does not practice only shamatha. There is also clarity, knowing: the knowledge of the nature of the mind, the way the mind really is. This knowledge sees the empty nature of the mind but also knows that it is not just emptiness alone. This is what is called the supreme emptiness, which means this is an emptiness from which everything can appear. For this self-knowing direct perception of the yogin, one uses the sixth consciousness, but not its conceptual aspect, with which one can gain only a conceptual comprehension. The nonconceptual mental consciousness used in meditation does not bring comprehension; it brings experience. Together with the experience of the true nature of mind by this nonconceptual sixth consciousness, bliss, clarity, and nonthought arise. One does not fall under the power of these experiences, because one has the direct perception of the nature of the mind. This is what occurs in the fourth type of direct perception, that of the yogin, when the nonconceptual sixth consciousness directly perceives the nature of the mind.

Next, *An Ocean of the Ultimate Meaning* describes how one proceeds in terms of these instructions. Gampopa had a student named Gomtsul, who was his nephew. Gomtsul in turn had a student named Lama Shang, who composed many instructions and songs. Lama Shang said that Mahamudra is instantaneous—it is a direct looking at the nature of the mind. Therefore, he said, to see Mahamudra as a progressive path is a delusion. But as we've seen, there are different kinds of practitioners: There are those who are the instantaneous kind, those who jump from level to level, and those who progress gradually. Most people are gradualists, and gradual progression is very stable. Therefore, Wangchuk Dorje said that it is not a contradiction to teach the path of Mahamudra in stages that accord with those practitioners who progress gradually.

The description of progress along the path is presented in terms of four yogas: (1) the yoga of one-pointedness, (2) the yoga of simplicity, or freedom from elaboration, (3) the yoga of one taste, and (4) the yoga of nonmeditation.

What is the result that we are trying to attain? We are trying to attain buddhahood. What is meant by buddhahood? In Tibetan the word for "buddha" is *sanggye*. It is made up of two syllables, *sang* and *gye*. *Sang* means purified. The mind has an empty essence and a nature of clarity; that is how it has always been. However, we don't recognize this true nature, and so we are in a state of delusion. This delusion, which is a fault that we need to eliminate, is composed of two kinds of ignorance: the obscuration of the defilements and the obscuration of knowledge. The obscuration of the defilements is directly harmful; the obscuration of knowledge is not, but it does prevent the final result. Purification serves to remove the two obscurations. This is *sang*, the first half of the word for buddha.

Purifying these faults results in the development of the qualities of buddhahood. This development is the meaning of the syllable *gye*, the second half of *sanggye*. The qualities that are developed are wisdom, love, and power. Wisdom is knowing the nature of all things as they truly are and knowing the entire multiplicity of phenomena. Love means love and compassion for all beings without exception. With this love and compassion comes the power of a buddha to benefit beings. All these qualities appear at buddhahood. Therefore, we have the word "buddha"—in Tibetan, *sanggye*.

We wish to attain the state of buddhahood, but we can't achieve it immediately. It is a gradual process of developing qualities and eliminating faults. The qualities we wish to attain are gradually attained, and the faults we wish to eliminate, like the obscurations of the defilements and of knowledge, are gradually eliminated. These obscurations can be either in manifest form or in the form of seeds. In an ordinary being, the faults are manifest, and we practice to overcome and diminish them. Through eliminating these faults to some extent, we are able to see the true nature of phenomena. The faults that are seeds are at the level of the *aryas*. Their practice is to uproot these seeds and to increase the clear vision of the true nature of phenomena. The complete removal of the seed faults constitutes the attainment of buddhahood.

This achievement of buddhahood has been attained. Shakyamuni Buddha appeared in this world, and afterward came many great masters and siddhas. In India there were Tilopa and Naropa; in Tibet, Marpa, Milarepa, and Gampopa. One may ask if their attainment is the same as that of the Buddha. Their realization is the same, but there is a difference in terms of their qualities. Shakyamuni Buddha was someone who had gathered the accumulation of merit for many aeons until he reached the state of a tenth-level bodhisattva, from which state he attained buddhahood. Because of this his body displayed the thirty-two major and eighty secondary signs of a great being, his speech had the sixty special qualities, and so on. The later masters were born as ordinary beings and attained buddhahood in one lifetime. They attained the same realization, but they didn't have the thirty-two major and eighty secondary signs, the sixty special qualities of speech, and so on. But in terms of what has to be attained and what has to be eliminated, their accomplishment was identical; they are inseparable from the Buddha.

Basically the path is the same, whether it is the path of the Vajrayana, the path of the ten levels of the bodhisattva, or the five paths. The Vajrayana path is swift, while the path of the sutras, that of traversing the ten *bhumis*, takes a very long time. That is the only difference between the two paths. Otherwise, they are the same.

In terms of progressing along the path in Vajrayana and Mahamudra, there are four yogas. First is the yoga of *one-pointedness*, in which one develops shamatha and vipashyana and they become very stable. Second, there is the yoga of *simplicity*, or freedom from conceptual elaboration, in which one sees the true nature of phenomena free from conceptual complication. Third, there is the yoga of *one taste*, in which everything is seen as having one nature, without likes or dislikes, without thoughts of good or bad, and so on. And finally, there is the yoga of *nonmeditation*, which is like the union of meditation and postmeditation. In the first three yogas, there is a distinction between meditation and the appearances in postmeditation. But in the yoga of nonmeditation, there is a blending of meditation and postmeditation. At this point, meditation in no way diminishes one's ability to benefit beings, and benefiting beings in no way diminishes one's meditation. There is no real thing to meditate upon. This is called the yoga of nonmeditation.

In the first yoga of one-pointedness, through shamatha and vipashyana one sees the true nature of mind with clarity and is able to rest in that state. In the state of one-pointedness, one has experiences of bliss, clarity, and nonthought. If one is habituated to this state for only short periods of time, it is called the lesser yoga of one-pointedness; if one is habituated to it for a longer time, then it is the middle level of one-pointedness; and if one is habituated to it for long periods, that is the greater one-pointedness. *An Ocean of the Ultimate Meaning* teaches in detail about the lesser, middle, and greater levels of each of the four yogas.

The second yoga is the yoga of simplicity, or freedom from elaboration. One maintains the one-pointed resting of the first yoga, and it becomes clearer and clearer until the one-pointedness is experienced free from attachment. One cultivates this state by viewing the mind in stillness and in movement. One realizes the innate wisdom of the nature of the mind and thereby realizes the nature of thoughts. In the yoga of one-pointedness, there is some realization of the nature of the mind, but it occurs primarily in the context of shamatha, whereas in the yoga of freedom from elaboration, one also realizes the nature of thoughts. One realizes that thoughts have no arising, abiding, or ceasing. One also has an understanding that phenomena are free from conceptual elaboration, which means that one is free from the conceptual elaboration of the extremes: One realizes that things are not existent, not nonexistent, not both, and not neither. This comprehension is not something conceptual or mentally fabricated—it is a direct understanding, a direct seeing. Even the meditation experiences that arise are seen as empty. The nature of one's knowing is revealed. The direct realization of the state of simplicity is similar to a skin or outer layer being pulled away. It's like discovering a treasure. There is the understanding of the empty nature of the mind and the empty nature of phenomena. As the clarity and power of one's meditation increase, one progresses through the lesser, medium, and greater levels of the yoga of simplicity.

As one proceeds beyond the level of simplicity, one attains the level of the yoga of one taste, in which there is freedom from likes and dislikes, from thoughts of good and bad, and so on. At the level of one taste, the nature of mind is seen, free from thought, and therefore, one's experience is pleasant. Thought and conceptualization make one's mental state uncomfortable. Here one sees the mind that is free from complication, and then one meditates directly upon this emptiness. With the mind free from conceptualization, one is able to meditate upon the movement of the mind as well as directly on appearances. In this way, one can remain in the pleasant state of one taste, in which one meditates directly on emptiness without any attachment to it. That is the state of one taste. Again there are lesser, medium, and greater stages as one progresses. At the level of simplicity, one sees emptiness, but there is still some attachment to it. At the level of one taste, there isn't just emptiness alone; emptiness is seen arising as interdependent phenomena.

Following the level of one taste is the final yoga of nonmeditation. At the levels of simplicity and one taste, one practices meditation and then arises from that into the postmeditation state; the two states of meditation and postmeditation are different. When one reaches the level of nonmeditation, there is a merging of meditation and postmeditation, so that when one is active and benefiting beings, one still maintains the state of meditation. In the state of nonmeditation, there is mindfulness and awareness, so there is no distraction. If one is in solitude, one is content, and if one is in the midst of many people, one is not distracted. As with all of the yogas, there are gradations. One begins with the lesser level of nonmeditation, and that develops and gets better and better until finally one attains the state of the great nonmeditation in which thoughts cause no change. As each of the four yogas has three stages, one can also say that there are twelve yogas.

We can compare the graduated path of the Mahamudra to the graduated path as taught in the sutras and ascertain how they correspond. In the sutras there is a succession of five paths. The stage of lesser one-pointedness corresponds to the lesser stage of the path of accumulation. On the path of accumulation, one accumulates merit and through that develops meditation. Eventually, one is able to gain a mentally created state of meditation. This is something that one's mind creates; it is not realization and experience. This state is said to be the path of juncture, the second path. The path of accumulation and the path of juncture are said to be equivalent to the yoga of one-pointedness.

In the yoga of simplicity, there is the direct insight into the empty nature of the mind. In the sutra tradition, on the path of juncture, one is meditating on a conceptual or generalized meaning of the nature of mind. It's not until one attains the third path, the path of seeing, that one has direct insight into the true nature. Thus, the path of seeing is equivalent to the yoga of simplicity.

It is taught in the sutra tradition that the first two paths of accumulation and juncture are paths of ordinary beings. From the path of seeing onward are the paths of the aryas, the enlightened beings who traverse the ten levels, from the first level, Joy, to the tenth level, the Cloud of Dharma. The path of seeing is the equivalent of the first bodhisattva level, Joy, in which one directly sees the true nature of phenomena. Is this seeing enough? No, it isn't, so there follows the fourth path, the path of meditation. Although one has removed the obstacles that prevented one from directly seeing the true nature of phenomena, one still has to eliminate all the tendencies accumulated throughout beginningless time, that is, we must eliminate the obscuration of knowledge. This is achieved on the path of meditation, which extends from the second bodhisattva level to the tenth. These nine bodhisattva levels comprise the path of meditation. In terms of all ten bodhisattva levels, the first seven are designated as impure, while the eighth, ninth, and tenth are called the pure bodhisattva levels.

The lesser level of the Mahamudra yoga of simplicity corresponds to the first bodhisattva level, as well as to the sutra path of seeing. If one achieves the medium and greater levels of simplicity, one has reached the sixth bodhisattva level. Then one enters the lesser level of one taste, which equates with the seventh bodhisattva level. The yoga of one taste extends from the seventh to the ninth bodhisattva levels. At the ninth bodhisattva level, one has reached the greater level of the yoga of one taste. Then, at the beginning of the tenth bodhisattva level, one is on the stage of the lesser yoga of nonmeditation. With the middle level of nonmeditation, one has completed the tenth bodhisattva level, in which one has gained the vajralike samadhi. Through that vajralike samadhi, one then achieves the state of buddhahood, which is the same as the greater state of nonmeditation. In that way, the four yogas of Mahamudra correspond with the levels and paths of the sutra tradition.

XIII

Attaining the Result

~:~

At the conclusion of the path, there is the attainment of the ultimate result, which is called the ultimate siddhi. There are two kinds of siddhi, ultimate and general. We can speak of either the attainment of the ultimate siddhi or the attainment of buddhahood. They are the same. One attains the state of buddhahood by proceeding through the twelve yogas of Mahamudra. At the level of greater non-meditation, one has attained buddhahood.

The attainment of the result means that one sees the nature of the mind, which is emptiness. In the sutra system, this empty nature of the mind is said to be like the expanse, or space, of phenomena, which in Sanskrit is called the *dharmadhatu*. This *dhatu*, or expanse (in Tibetan the word is *ying*), is such that anything can appear within it, anything can arise. This is the emptiness aspect of the nature of the mind. The other aspect is the wisdom aspect, which in Sanskrit is *jñana*. This is the wisdom that sees the nature of things as they are and also sees all the multiplicity of things. This wisdom can see the true nature of the mind. In the Mahamudra, this wisdom and this expanse, or emptiness, are one; they are indivisible. It's not that one has only space, or emptiness, without wisdom, or only wisdom without emptiness—they are one taste. This is the ground, the basis, of Mahamudra. In terms of this ground Mahamudra, when the nature of mind is looked at, it isn't seen as just an inert emptiness or a state of dullness. There is clarity and wisdom. There is the indivisibility of this space, this emptiness, with clarity and wisdom. This is the basis. How does one realize that? One realizes it through a union of shamatha and vipashyana. Through shamatha the mind becomes still and stable, but in this case it isn't mere stability. There is also vipashyana, which sees the nature of the mind. In that way, one gains the supreme accomplishment of buddhahood.

In attaining the supreme result through the practice of shamatha and vipashyana, one gains the understanding of the nature of the mind, the essence of the mind. This is the dharmakaya, which is complete benefit for oneself. Through looking at the nature of the mind, there is the development of wisdom, which becomes completely manifest. And that which is to be eliminated, ignorance, is completely purified. Thus, one attains the dharmakaya, in which everything that needs to be realized is realized and everything that needs to be eliminated is eliminated. In this supreme result, one does not just remain as the dharmakaya, for the supreme result is both the dharmakaya and the form kayas. Though one has attained the dharmakaya, there are still other beings who have not yet realized it. For their benefit there is the appearance of the *rupakayas*, or form kayas, of which there are two kinds: the sambhogakaya and the *nirmanakaya*. To those with pure perception appear the sambhogakayas, the buddhas that dwell in the pure realms. Only beings who have pure perception are able to see the sambhogakaya buddhas. For those beings who do not have pure perception, the supreme nirmanakaya will appear at certain times: A buddha will appear in the world with the major and minor signs of a great being and teach the Dharma to beings. Thus, one attains the dharmakaya to benefit oneself and the rupakayas to accomplish benefit for others. Through the rupakayas there is continuous activity, the four kinds of buddha activity that benefit sentient beings. Thus, there is the dharmakaya, and there are also the sambhogakaya and nirmanakaya, the latter two forming the rupakaya. In this way, it can be said that there are either two or three kayas.

The Dharma has been taught and has spread in this world, but what was its source? The source was Shakyamuni Buddha, a supreme nirmanakaya, who appeared in this world and gave the Dharma teachings. In an impure world with ordinary beings, the activity of a sambhogakaya buddha does not occur, and therefore we have had the appearance of the supreme nirmanakaya of Shakyamuni Buddha.

The Mahamudra lineage comes from Vajradhara, Tilopa, Naropa, Marpa, Milarepa, and so on. Who was Vajradhara? Shakyamuni Buddha is the buddha of this world, and he is a nirmanakaya appearance. Therefore, as a nirmanakaya, he passed into nirvana. This means that his body passed away, but not his mind. As a nirmanakaya, he had a physical form, and that form had to pass away, but his mind, with its compassion and wisdom for beings, did not pass away into nirvana. His mind is always present. But it is not possible to meet the mind of the Buddha, so there is the manifestation of the sambhogakaya. Beings with pure perception are able to encounter the sambhogakaya, who is continuously teaching in a pure realm, whereas a nirmanakaya, like Shakyamuni Buddha, teaches only at a certain time in the world of ordinary beings. The sambhogakaya Vajradhara is depicted in paintings as a buddha who is blue in color, holds a vajra and bell, and sits in the vajra posture. Shakyamuni Buddha and Vajradhara appear to be different, but in essence they are the same. In terms of mind, in terms of their wisdom and compassion, they are inseparable.

A sambhogakaya buddha teaches continuously and never passes away into nirvana. The great bodhisattvas are able to receive teachings directly from Vajradhara. A great master such as Tilopa was able to receive teachings from great bodhisattvas, but also as a result of his own realization and experience, he received instructions directly from the sambhogakaya buddha Vajradhara. Receiving teachings from Vajradhara is the same as receiving teachings from Shakyamuni Buddha. Therefore, the Mahamudra lineage was transmitted from Vajradhara through Tilopa.

As the Mahamudra lineage came from Vajradhara through Tilopa, one might think that Shakyamuni Buddha did not teach Mahamudra, but that is not the case. Shakyamuni Buddha taught Mahamudra in the *Mahamudra Tantra* (*The Tantra of the Stainless Bindu of the Mahamudra*). If Shakyamuni Buddha taught Mahamudra, what did Vajradhara teach? Vajradhara gave the blessing for this practice of Mahamudra. That blessing gives us the ability to develop the experience and realization of the Mahamudra teachings. In this way, the Mahamudra lineage derives from Vajradhara, and Tilopa passed on the lineage of the blessings of Mahamudra.

PART FOUR

THE SUPPLEMENTARY
TEACHINGS

XIV

Further Explanations of Mahamudra

Having explained the preliminaries, the main practice, and the conclusion—including enhancing the result, removing obstacles to practice, proceeding along the path, and gaining the final result—at this point in *An Ocean of the Ultimate Meaning*, Wangchuk Dorje adds a supplementary teaching of five points in order to further one's understanding of Mahamudra.

THE NATURE OF MAHAMUDRA

The first point identifies the nature of Mahamudra—that is, what is meant by "Mahamudra." There are many names that can be given for Mahamudra. One can say "the Great Middle Way." One can say "Dzogchen." One can say "Prajñaparamita." All these different terms, which have slightly different meanings, are names for the same thing. The Great Middle Way means it is in the middle, free from all extremes. Dzogchen, the Great Perfection, means it is totally complete. Mahamudra, the Great Seal, means it pervades everything. Prajñaparamita, the perfection of wisdom, means the wisdom that is totally complete. All these are different names for the same thing, and the meaning is inexpressible in words or thought. One cannot really say it is this thing, it is nothing, it is empty, and so forth. If Mahamudra cannot be expressed in words and thought, how can it be taught? It is taught in the same way that one points out the moon in the sky. If someone doesn't know where the moon is or even that there is a moon in the sky, you can point to it with your finger and say, "There it is." You point with your finger, but there is no moon at the tip of your finger. If someone follows where your finger is pointing, the moon can be seen. But someone who just looks at the end of your finger is not going to see the moon.

In the same way, by following the instructions that teach Mahamudra, eventually one will be able to gain realization. If one merely listens to the words—"Mahamudra is this," "Mahamudra is emptiness," and so on—one will not know it; one will not see it. But one *can* see this true nature, and even though one will not be able to express it in words or conceive of it in one's mind, one will have the experience and understanding of Mahamudra. Although it cannot really be expressed through the relative medium of words and thought, it is through words and thought that one gains the insight of the ultimate meaning.

Where is Mahamudra taught? In the sutra system, the Buddha's teachings are divided into three sections called the Tripitaka; and in addition to these three sections, there are also the tantras. In the sutra system, within the Tripitaka, one finds Mahamudra taught sometimes in the Perfection of Wisdom sutras and sometimes in other sutras. Also, the Mahamudra teachings are found within the tantras that were taught by the Buddha. Primarily, however, the Mahamudra practice instructions are given by lamas based on their experience in meditation.

Lama Shang says this dharmakaya Mahamudra is something highly renowned and very famous. But what is this Mahamudra? It is the recognition of one's own mind. We all have a mind that thinks all sorts of things, but if we can recognize the nature of our mind, then that is the recognition of Mahamudra. Thus, just through realizing the nature of our own mind, we will realize the meaning that is taught in the sutras and tantras. That is the identification of the nature of Mahamudra.

CATEGORIES OF MAHAMUDRA

There are three categories of Mahamudra: ground Mahamudra, path Mahamudra, and result Mahamudra.

Ground Mahamudra

First there is ground Mahamudra. This is what one wishes to realize, and it is within all beings. Mahamudra is present within all beings, all the way from the Buddha down to a little insect on a blade of grass. Even that tiny little insect has Mahamudra. It is not that Mahamudra is something really good so that only the Buddha possesses it properly; it's not that the Buddha's Mahamudra is good but ordinary human beings' Mahamudra is not; and it's not that the Mahamudra of the Buddha is vast while the Mahamudra of ordinary human beings is small. It's not any of these things. Mahamudra is within all beings, and it is exactly the same within all beings.

Although Mahamudra is present within us, we have not understood it, and so we have a misconception of our true nature. It's as if we have made an error, like mistaking a rope for a snake. There is a rope lying on the ground, but we have misperceived it and think it is a snake. We are in delusion. We might think that Mahamudra sounds too easy and so we don't trust in it. That too is a misconception. Regardless of whether we have mistaken it or feel no confidence in it, Mahamudra is still within all beings. This is ground Mahamudra.

Path Mahamudra

We now come to what is called path Mahamudra. Within all beings is the ground Mahamudra that we need to realize. This is the realization that the mind is empty, but this empty nature of mind is not something that we have created with our meditation or understanding. The mind has always had this empty nature. We also need to realize the unceasing clarity of the mind, but again, this unceasing clarity is not something that we create through meditation. It is something that has primordially been the nature of the mind. We need a method to realize this ground Mahamudra, which is the nature of the mind; that method is path Mahamudra, which is all of the methods and instructions that are given. One engages in the practices of shamatha and vipashyana. Within vipashyana there are three kinds of practice: viewing the mind in stillness, viewing the mind in movement, and viewing appearances. In this way, one comes to know what was previously unknown. From these path instructions, one gains experience and learns how to increase that experience so that it becomes clearer and clearer. There are also the methods for enhancing the result of the practice and eliminating obstacles, and through these one progresses along the path and finally attains the result. This teaching on the methods to realize ground Mahamudra *is* path Mahamudra.

Devotion is very important for path Mahamudra. Götsangpa wrote that faith and devotion are of the greatest importance. This is not referring to blind faith but to a faith based on a clear understanding of the nature of the teachings. Through understanding the teachings, one develops faith and devotion in them. If we look at the life story of Naropa, we see how he underwent so many hardships as a student of Tilopa. It might seem as if Naropa's actions were done out of blind faith, but they were not. Naropa understood that Tilopa had instructions that could bring buddhahood within one lifetime. He had the certainty that Tilopa's instructions would bring the ultimate result and that with Tilopa he could realize those instructions and attain that result himself. Knowing this, he had faith and devotion in Tilopa and his instructions, so he was not just acting out of blind faith.

We can also read Milarepa's life story and see the hardships that he went through in following Marpa's instructions. Again, it might seem as if he were acting out of blind faith, but Milarepa had the understanding and conviction not only that Marpa had the profound instructions but also that, through skillful means and blessings, Marpa could bring him to the ultimate result. Therefore, he had faith and devotion in Marpa. Wangchuk Dorje emphasizes that faith and devotion are of the greatest importance, but this faith and devotion come from understanding, not from blind faith.

Path Mahamudra is described in terms of view, meditation, and conduct. A quote by Gampopa presents this especially clearly. Gampopa says that the mind is clear but there is nothing to grasp; it is like space. In other words, there is clarity in the mind, but in this clarity there is nothing that one can grasp or identify. It is like space in that one cannot fall into an extreme of thinking of it as being good or bad, of being self or me. There is just a clarity, without any extremes of identification. Gampopa says that this is the view: The mind knows itself and is self-clear like a mirror. There is the clarity of self-knowing, which never fluctuates. It's not that sometimes it's clear and sometimes it isn't. The nature of the mind is always the same. Having that self-knowing clarity without any fluctuation is the meditation. The mind is left in an uncontrived state, natural and relaxed, like a baby, without any cessation or accomplishment. That is the conduct.

Result Mahamudra

Ground Mahamudra is already present; path Mahamudra is the various practices of shamatha and vipashyana; and these enable the ground Mahamudra to manifest as result Mahamudra. In result Mahamudra, appearances are seen as having the nature of the dharmakaya, and the nature of the mind is seen to be empty but with unceasing clarity.

One looks at the nature of the mind and sees that it is empty and has no reality of its own, that there is nothing to be identified, and that it is free from conceptual complication. This means that one sees that the mind has no existence, but that does not mean that it is nonexistent. There isn't that conceptual complication—that is, one is free from its having to have existence or nonexistence. Usually, one thinks of existence and nonexistence as opposites, so if there is no existence, then there must be nonexistence, and vice versa. But the nature of the mind is empty and beyond conceptual elaboration; therefore, it is the expanse of emptiness.

Seeing emptiness in this way is the arising of the dharmakaya, the attainment of the dharmakaya. This emptiness of the mind is not a mere emptiness in which there is nothing whatsoever. It is not a material emptiness, like the deadness of a stone, with no knowledge or awareness. Although the nature of the mind is emptiness, there is self-knowing; the mind knows itself. There is clarity, so the mind sees itself, knows itself, realizes itself. This self-knowing clarity can arise as a variety of appearances, just as is said in the Vajradhara lineage prayer: "It is nothing whatsoever, but anything whatsoever can arise from it." In this way, the nature of the mind is emptiness together with this self-knowing clarity. Seeing the emptiness is the dharmakaya; the self-knowing clarity, which can arise as anything whatsoever, is the sambhogakaya.

One sees the essence of the mind as the dharmakaya, and the nature of clarity as the sambhogakaya. The clarity is like a seed for the appearance of the sambhogakaya forms. The mind's emptiness has an unceasing luminosity, or radiance, that is able to manifest as a variety of externally appearing phenomena. The analogy often given is that of a dream. Although there is nothing really present in a dream, things appear that seem to be external phenomena. In dreams we see mountains, forests, houses, friends, and so on—yet they don't exist. And even though they don't exist, they still appear as objects of perception. For us who are in the impure state, in samsara, appearances are impure phenomena. With the realization of the emptiness of the mind, external forms will still appear but not as impure forms; instead, they will manifest as activities that benefit beings. This is the nirmanakaya, such as the supreme nirmanakaya that guides all beings. In this way, one attains all three kayas.

These three kayas are already present and complete within the nature of one's own mind: The dharmakaya is the empty nature; the sambhogakaya is the nature of clarity; and the nirmanakaya is the arising of various appearances. These are present in our mind, but we have not yet been able to recognize them. There is the analogy of a sesame seed. Within the sesame seed there is sesame oil, but unless the seed is crushed, the oil doesn't appear. Even before the seed is crushed, the sesame oil is still present in the seed. In the same way, the three kayas are present in one's mind, but they do not manifest until one recognizes the nature of the mind. It is like an emerald contained within a stone. We cannot see the emerald because it's hidden, but by removing the surrounding stone we can expose the emerald. In the same way, the three kayas have always been present within the mind but are not manifest. Because they are naturally present in the mind as it is, without one's having to change the mind in any way, these qualities gradually become manifest through one's practice.

Rangjung Dorje taught that the five wisdoms are present in the nature of the mind. The five wisdoms are the dharmadhatu wisdom, the mirrorlike wisdom, the equality wisdom, the discriminating wisdom, and the accomplishing wisdom. With the attainment of the result, that is, when one sees the nature of the mind, the eight consciousnesses transform into the five wisdoms. When one sees the empty essence, this empty aspect, which is the dharmadhatu wisdom, is manifest. When one sees the clarity aspect, this is the mirrorlike wisdom. The empty aspect is the dharmadhatu, and the clarity aspect is the mirrorlike wisdom. Clarity and emptiness exist together. Emptiness does not prevent clarity, and clarity does not prevent emptiness. These two coexist equally, which is the equality wisdom.

When we have the dharmadhatu wisdom, the mirrorlike wisdom, and the equality wisdom, they remain clear and distinct; they do not blend or merge. This is the discriminating wisdom. There is clarity, and there is emptiness. Clarity does not become confused with emptiness, nor emptiness with clarity. They are seen distinctly. Finally, the wisdom of emptiness and the wisdom of clarity are distinct and are naturally present. They are not present due to change or artifice but due to the natural presence, or natural accomplishment, of the wisdoms. This is the accomplishing wisdom. When one gains the result of Mahamudra, these five wisdoms naturally arise.

Mahamudra is taught in the tantras. There are four levels of tantra: *kriya*, *charya*, yoga, and highest yoga tantra. It is in the highest yoga tantra, the *anuttara* tantra, that Mahamudra is taught. Anuttara tantra is of three kinds: the father tantras, mother tantras, and nondual tantras. One may ask what the difference is, if any, between these three types of tantra that teach Mahamudra. The teachings within the mother tantras are primarily concerned with bliss and the indivisibility of bliss and the empty nature—the union of bliss and emptiness. The teachings within the father tantras are primarily on clarity—the union of clarity and emptiness. And it is primarily in the nondual tantras that both of these—bliss and emptiness, and clarity and emptiness—are taught equally. While the father tantras, for example, emphasize clarity, the nondual tantras present the teaching on the union of knowledge and emptiness. Thus, Mahamudra is the ultimate teaching of all three classes of highest yoga tantra.

THE MEANING OF THE WORD

The next point concerns the meaning of the word "Mahamudra," which in Tibetan is *chag gya chenpo*. The Tibetan term is made up of three parts: *chag*, *gya*, and *chenpo*. The real meaning of the first syllable, *chag*, is emptiness. The word *chag* means something that removes all impurity. The term *chag* is also used for the hand. One refers to the deity's *chag*, the deity's hand, because the deity is able to eliminate the suffering and ignorance of beings. So *chag* means hand, and it also means purifying. In the term *chag gya chenpo*, *chag* represents emptiness. Again, this is not making something empty that was not already empty. One is recognizing the empty nature that was always there, and through that one dispels suffering and the defilements. If a defilement arises and one is able to see its nature, then one can realize its nature; and when one realizes the empty nature of a defilement, then that defilement ceases. It is the same with any suffering. If we can see the nature of the suffering, then we can realize its empty nature. If we can realize the empty nature of suffering, then that suffering will cease to harm us. Therefore, in *chag gya chenpo*, *chag* has the meaning of emptiness.

The syllable *gya*, which means "seal," represents liberation from the phenomena of samsara. Emptiness is not a powerless emptiness; through it one is able to achieve liberation from samsara. The cause of samsara is ignorance. Because of ignorance there are defilements, and because of defilements there is the accumulation of karma, which results in the phenomena of samsara and its sufferings. The realization of Mahamudra eliminates the cause, which is ignorance. Therefore, one becomes liberated from all the phenomena and characteristics of samsara. The second syllable, *gya*, refers to the ability to attain liberation from samsara upon seeing the true nature.

Next is the word *chenpo,* meaning "great." Along with the emptiness aspect of the nature of the mind, there is clarity; there are appearances. In terms of relative phenomena, as ordinary beings we think that if there are appearances, there cannot be emptiness, and if there is emptiness, there cannot be appearances. We think that if there is clarity, there cannot be emptiness; or if there is emptiness, there cannot be clarity. We think of these aspects as opposites. But Mahamudra realization is not confined to one side or the other; it is something that pervades emptiness, clarity, and appearance. For that reason, it is called great. That is the meaning of *chenpo,* or the *maha* of Mahamudra.

JOINING WITH COEMERGENCE

Next, Wangchuk Dorje speaks of the application of innateness. This means that whether one is talking about the union of clarity and emptiness, or awareness and emptiness, and so forth, these are coemergent, that is, they are innately born together. We are not talking about something that was not already present. It is not the case that there is clarity or emptiness when one meditates but that these are absent when one is not meditating. These qualities of clarity and emptiness are innate to the mind. One might ask, when were they born together? When did they coemerge? When one looks at the nature of the mind, it is empty, so there was never any time when they were born, when they first emerged. The nature of the mind and its qualities are said to have been born together, to be coemergent. Although these qualities are already present in the mind, we will not recognize this innate nature without engaging in specific methods. We have to receive the instructions in order to see the innate nature. This is called union with that which is innate, or joining with coemergence.

What is the difference between Mahamudra and this joining with coemergence? There is a quotation from Gampopa given in response to a question by Pagmo Drupa concerning this difference. Gampopa said that Mahamudra is the primordial, naturally present nature of all phenomena. So Mahamudra is the natural state, and joining with coemergence is applying oneself to seeing that true nature. Mahamudra is the true nature, and joining with coemergence is the method used to realize it.

GAINING THE ULTIMATE RESULT

Through the practice of Mahamudra one can attain the ultimate result. First one proceeds through the four yogas, and ultimately one attains the state of buddhahood. Through practice, some people may gain some experience of Mahamudra meditation or gain some stabil-

ity in Mahamudra practice. Even if one does not achieve buddhahood in this lifetime through this practice, it still has a great benefit
and purpose. Even just developing an aspiration toward Mahamudra
has great benefit and purpose. We have gained a human existence,
and through Mahamudra practice we can make this human existence
meaningful, so it doesn't matter whether one immediately gains experience from Mahamudra or not. Through this practice one establishes a tendency and an aspiration that will eventually lead to the
ultimate result. Thus, whether one has experience or simply has faith
in Mahamudra, one will eventually attain benefit for oneself and,
through that, benefit for all other beings. Therefore, engaging in Mahamudra practice is very beneficial and has a great purpose. Even just
hearing these teachings on Mahamudra has great benefit and purpose.

Afterword

Buddhism has not been present in North America for very long, because America is separated by the great oceans from the original place of the Buddha's teachings. These teachings were introduced here at a much later time, and the Vajrayana teachings in particular were introduced even later. People are very fortunate to be able to practice the Dharma. The Buddha's activity always occurs at the right time. People wish to meet the Dharma and hear about it; they develop faith and conviction in the Dharma and wish to practice; and they practice free from doubt and wrong views. All this is a sign of practicing the Dharma well. Sometimes there are favorable conditions for practice, with no adverse circumstances, and at those times one can practice with diligence. At other times conditions may not be favorable; there may be adverse circumstances. During such times one shouldn't think, "I'm very unfortunate, and I'm not able to practice the Dharma," because merely having entered the Dharma is an extremely fortunate circumstance. Even if one isn't able to practice with diligence, one is fortunate. Whatever the circumstances, one is not unfortunate. It was the Buddha, not I, who said this.

The Buddha described different situations of good fortune. If someone really has faith and conviction in the Dharma, then great benefit comes from that, and that person is very fortunate. Another person might have a little faith or belief in the Dharma—perhaps only enough to put up one hand in homage, while thinking, "Well, it seems like it's probably a good thing to do." The Buddha said that someone who does only that much is also very fortunate, and great benefit will result. Someone with only enough faith to raise one hand in homage creates the tendency for the Dharma, which will have a future result. This will develop and become stronger and clearer so that eventually that person will accomplish their own benefit and then be able to benefit other beings. Benefiting oneself and benefiting others is the practice of the Dharma.

The Buddha also spoke of the benefit of relating to a place where people are practicing the Dharma and meditating well. Someone might think, "I must go to that place to get teachings and instructions," and take one step in that direction, but then some adverse circumstance might arise so that the person is unable to proceed. Even so, that person is very fortunate to have taken just one step with a positive motivation toward that place of Dharma. Because of that good motivation, that person will attain the ultimate result in the future.

To be able to practice with faith and devotion, with diligence, enthusiasm, and interest, and without any doubts or wrong views is very fortunate and beneficial. If in the future your circumstances are adverse, do not feel disheartened, depressed, or saddened. You are still very fortunate. And when favorable conditions arise, you should not waste the opportunity but take advantage of the time and apply yourself to practice.

If each day you can rest in the state of shamatha meditation—a simple, uncomplicated state, maintaining mindfulness and awareness—this is very beneficial. You may think, "I need to be in solitude," but one can't always be in a quiet place. In fact, it's actually better to meditate in a busy place that isn't solitary. At first it may be difficult to practice, but by continuing to meditate in that place, one will gradually develop a good meditation experience. This can be even better than practicing in solitude. When one has the time and opportunity, one can practice in solitude, but when one doesn't, then one practices while being engaged in one's work, while traveling, and so on. Maintaining mindfulness and awareness and continuing with meditation practice amid the circumstances of a busy life can give rise to a special experience. This can have a very beneficial result.

Sometimes in our life we have times of happiness. When we have a period of happiness, we shouldn't have attachment to that state or be distracted by it. If instead we can turn our mind inward and meditate on the nature, the essence, this will be beneficial. Sometimes we have times of unhappiness and suffering. At such times, instead of being tormented and overcome by suffering, we can rest in meditation. This will be beneficial for our present circumstances and also for the ultimate realization that can be attained. Sometimes we become sick and experience physical pain. If we can rest in meditation when experiencing illness and pain, this will be beneficial both in terms of our present experience and for the future. Therefore, whatever the circumstances, whether we are happy or sad, it is beneficial to be able to maintain mindfulness, awareness, and attentiveness in cultivating and maintaining meditation.

The Mahamudra teachings have been given by the great masters and siddhas of the past. Some have taught Mahamudra in the form of texts, some in the form of practice instructions, and some in the form of *dohas*, or songs of realization. In singing these songs, the great siddhas expressed their own joy in the practice of Mahamudra. The siddhas would sometimes sing these songs to large groups of people— rich and poor, studied and illiterate—in order to benefit others. They sang not to boast but with the motivation of wishing to help others and to express their joy at the benefit of Mahamudra practice to themselves and to others. Thus, Mahamudra is a very special method that can bring much benefit to others, and therefore I ask you to practice Mahamudra as much as you can in the future.

In the Vajrayana tradition, there are many different methods that one can use, and if one has the opportunity, the aspiration, and the interest to do these practices, one is very fortunate. But sometimes people don't have that opportunity. People are very busy. Today, unlike in the past, people have so much to do. On the one hand, it's true that we can't live as if this were the fifth or sixth century. At the same time, we can't abandon the Dharma, thinking that it doesn't belong in the twenty-first century. What we can do is practice Mahamudra, which is very easy and beneficial. We can do this meditation while doing our work. When you are working at your job, you can be meditating and doing Mahamudra at the same time. In this way, you aren't abandoning the Dharma. You are behaving in a way appropriate to the times and also practicing the Dharma. In this way, Mahamudra is very beneficial.

For example, Tilopa worked as a sesame seed grinder. He meditated on the nature of the mind as he pounded the seeds. He attained the accomplishment of Mahamudra and became a siddha. Having attained the ultimate accomplishment, he rose into the sky up to a height of seven palm trees, holding his little sesame seed pounder, and he sang a song about pounding sesame seeds. He sang that inside the sesame seeds there is the sesame oil, but if you don't pound them, you won't get the oil out. But because the oil is in the seeds, if you pound them, it will come out. In the same way, the nature of the mind is within us, but if we don't do anything about it, then we stay in the state of delusion and relative appearances. But just as the oil can be extracted from the seeds, this true nature of the mind can become manifest. We have this true nature of the mind, and it can be realized. Therefore, we shouldn't think, "I can't realize it," or "There's nothing to be realized." Nor should we think, "There is this nature of the mind to be realized, but I don't have time," and then forget about it. Instead, if we can do our work, practice within meditation sessions, and practice in the postmeditation period, then the experience of seeing the true nature of the mind can develop. This is what we should do. This is how we should practice.

Notes

2. ESSENTIAL POINTS OF THE MAIN MEDITATION

1. The eight consciousnesses are not explained in *An Ocean of the Ultimate Meaning*, but it is useful in the practice of meditation to understand how the mind appears and how it actually is. [Khenchen Thrangu]
2. In the Hinayana teachings, there are only six consciousnesses. The *Abhidharmakosha* (*Treasury of the Abhidharma*) by Vasubandhu is a principal text of the Hinayana that presents these teachings. The *Abhidharmasamuccaya* (*Compendium of the Abhidharma*) by Asanga is a Mahayana treatise in which eight consciousnesses are taught. [KT]
3. There are two kinds of objects: objects that appear clearly and vividly to the six consciousnesses and objects that reside in the ground consciousness as latencies. When we perceive things in a room, there are also many other things outside the room that we cannot perceive. Where are they? They are in the ground consciousness, not as objects but as latencies. When we leave the room, then the room and the things inside it remain in our ground consciousness, since they are no longer appearing to any of the six consciousnesses.

   The ground consciousness is vast in terms of the objects contained within it. The whole world is contained in the ground consciousness in the form of latencies. We can go anywhere in this world, and that place will appear, will become a vivid appearance, because everywhere we can go is already present as a latency in the ground consciousness. [KT]
4. The five wisdoms are explained in chapter 14 on page 173–74.

3. SETTLING THE UNSETTLED MIND

1. The true nature of the eighth consciousness is the inseparability of clarity and emptiness. Ordinarily, the clarity aspect of this consciousness

is too strong, too intense, and it is grasped or recognized, while the emptiness aspect is not recognized. Therefore, there is delusion. If the emptiness aspect is realized, that is buddha nature. But when the clarity aspect of the ground consciousness is too strong, it is not recognized as empty, and therefore it is grasped and given an identity. That is what is called ignorance. One might say that ignorance is a state of not knowing, of being totally obscured and dark, but ignorance is not really a state of darkness. Really ignorance is about clarity—it's this misidentification of clarity. It's like a state of clarity in which one sees the entire variety of phenomena.

Purifying the eighth consciousness requires purifying all the karmic tendencies that are within it. But when you look at the nature of mind, you get a sudden, instantaneous glimpse of buddha nature. Having experienced that glimpse, you need to make it more and more stable. By doing so you are gradually purifying the eighth consciousness. [KT]

2. The *ushnisha* and *urna* are, respectively, the protuberance on top of the Buddha's head and the curl of hair between his eyebrows.

5. ENHANCING STABILITY IN MEDITATION

1. In relative terms, in both the meditation and postmeditation periods, the negative has to be eliminated and the positive cultivated. But in terms of developing realization and experience, it doesn't matter whether good thoughts or bad thoughts arise. One simply maintains the stability of meditation. [KT]

8. CUTTING THROUGH THE ROOT

1. The view of the Chittamatra school is discussed in more detail in chapter 9.

9. DEVELOPING CERTAINTY IN THE UNION OF EMPTINESS AND AWARENESS

1. The difference between vipashyana and realization is that vipashyana, or insight (Tib. *lhag thong*, seeing clearly), is the first arising of

the experience of clearly seeing the nature of the mind. The first insight appears vividly, and one sustains it so that it becomes stable; that experience subsequently becomes realization. Realization is the stability and clarity of the insight of vipashyana. [KT]

2. Anger causes much harm, but in these instructions it is important, because its nature is easily realized. From among the defilements, anger is the easiest to recognize. Attachment is somewhat less easy to recognize but is easier to recognize than ignorance. [KT]

10. ENHANCING THE RESULT

1. The nature of the mind is pure, but we have a perception of impurity. We need to transform this into a perception of purity. Therefore, we meditate that we are the pure form of the deity. Even if we cannot do it well, this practice still creates the tendency that will develop into a perception of purity in the future. Visualizing the deity and focusing on the deity's body and features will also help one to develop shamatha meditation. In addition, developing an awareness of the purity of the visualized deity helps one to develop vipashyana. This awareness helps in the development of pure perception and clarity. The dissolving of the deity—when everything disappears into emptiness and one rests in that state—helps one to develop vipashyana, the insight into emptiness, as well. This is the practice of the completion stage. Resting in the completion stage is beneficial for the creation stage. The practice of the creation stage also helps the progress of the completion stage. They help each other. [KT]

2. The reason for meditating on the true nature and the reason for practicing deity meditation are actually the same. In meditating on the true nature of the mind, we see that it is devoid of any real nature, that it is empty; as a result, wisdom arises. In the Middle Way, this is called emptiness, and in the Shentong tradition, this is buddha nature. In practicing deity meditation, we realize that all beings have buddha nature and therefore have the power to manifest the buddha body. Instead of having impure perception, we develop the pure perception of pure appearances. At present, we are attached to impure appearances and perceptions and so are unable to eliminate what needs to be eliminated. But through meditation on

ourselves as the pure form of the deity in a pure realm, this pure perception will become clearer and clearer, and we will eliminate impure appearances more and more. This elimination of what needs to be eliminated enables wisdom to arise. [KT]

11. ELIMINATING OBSTACLES

1. That is, dullness due to the time of day.

12. PROCEEDING ALONG THE PATH

1. This is not taught in *An Ocean of the Ultimate Meaning,* but it has been presented by the third Karmapa, Rangjung Dorje. As part of his teaching on Mahamudra and the true nature of mind, the third Karmapa included two additional short texts. One of these texts explains the consciousnesses and the wisdoms and the distinctions between them, as well as how the mind is when it is deluded and when it is not. The other short text, which teaches about buddha nature, is called *The Teaching on the Essence.* Buddha nature is taught in the *Uttaratantra Shastra* written by Maitreyanatha and is also taught at length in *The Seven Vajra Points.* The third Karmapa presents this topic in a very clear way and shows in a few concise sections how buddha nature is actually present within all beings. In the text on differentiating consciousness and wisdom, he teaches specifically on the eight consciousnesses. [KT]

2. There are two forms of the mental (sixth) consciousness: conceptual and nonconceptual. Nonconceptual direct mental perception arises immediately subsequent to a sensory consciousness. For example, if there is a visual consciousness, it is immediately followed by this nonconceptual mental consciousness, which serves as the connection between the mental consciousness and the sensory consciousness. Then there is the conceptual mental consciousness. This does not directly perceive external objects, but within it all different kinds of thoughts and concepts arise. Here resides the illusion that the concept and the object are one. There is the outer appearance as well as the conception of that appearance—good, bad, names, and so on—and these are mixed into one, so that thought and appearance merge. This happens when a word and its sound are mixed

with an object. There is the word that one has heard and there is the external object that one has perceived, and one's mind mixes the word with the perception. In that way, the conceptual mental consciousness is continuously busy doing a great number of different things. These mental processes are described in the pramana studies of epistemology and logic. The purpose of this type of study is to understand how the mind mixes names and appearances and how it perceives things in a deluded way. [KT]

Glossary

ABHIDHARMA (*chos mngon pa*)   One of the three collections of the Buddha's teachings, along with the Vinaya and the sutras, that compose the Tripitaka. In the Tibetan canon the Abhidharma consists entirely of commentarial literature, with only sutras and Vinaya texts comprising the collected teachings of the Buddha itself. The Abhidharma is a systematic presentation of the basic constituents of the Buddha's teachings.

AFFLICTED CONSCIOUSNESS (*nyon yid*; Skt. *klistajñana*)   The seventh consciousness; a subtle, pervasive sense of "I" that is continuously present. See also eight consciousnesses.

AGGREGATES   See five aggregates.

AIRS   See nadi, vayu, and bindu.

ALAYA (*kun gzhi*)   The Tibetan term means "the basis of all." When its nature is not recognized, it is called the *alayavijñana*, or ground consciousness. When it is recognized, it is the ground wisdom. See also Ground consciousness; Eight consciousnesses.

AMITABHA   See five buddhas.

AMOGHASIDDHI   See five buddhas.

ARHAT (*dgra bcom pa*)   The Sanskrit literally means "worthy one," but the Tibetan term literally means "foe destroyer," based upon the Sanskrit Nirukta tradition of creative etymologies. In the Mahayana tradition, it has come to mean those who have achieved the nirvana that is the final goal of the Hinayana path. While still living, they are called "arhats with residue," referring to the physical body, which is the result of residual karma. When they have passed into nirvana, they are called "arhats without residue." In that state of quiescence, they are no longer able to help beings. According to the *Lotus Sutra*, the Buddha eventually awakens them from this state so that they can proceed to full buddhahood.

ARYA (*'phags pa*)   "The noble ones." Those who have attained the first bodhisattva bhumi and above.

AVALOKITESHVARA (*spyan ras gzigs*)   The bodhisattva of compassion.

AYATANAS (*skye mched*)   The Sanskrit means "basis," while the Tibetan literally means "birth and development." These are the twelve bases of perception, consisting of the six sense faculties (sight, hearing, smell, taste, touch, and the mental faculty) and the six sense objects (sights, sounds, smells, tastes, bodily sensations, and mental objects).

BARDO (*bar do*)   "The intermediate state." The term principally refers to the time between death and rebirth, which is commonly subdivided into three bardos. It is also used for various other periods, such as between birth and death, or periods of sleep or meditation.

BENKAR JAMPAL ZANGPO (fifteenth century)   A disciple of the sixth Karmapa, Tongwa Donden, and a teacher of the seventh Karmapa. Benkar Jampal Zangpo composed the Vajradhara Mahamudra lineage prayer.

BHUMI   See ten bhumis.

BINDU   See nadi, vayu, and bindu.

BODHICHITTA (*byang chub kyi sems*)   Literally, "enlightenment mind." Bodhichitta has two aspects. Relative bodhichitta is the aspiration to attain enlightenment for the benefit of all sentient beings. Ultimate bodhichitta is the realization of emptiness.

BODHISATTVA (*byang chub sems dpa'*)   A practitioner of the Mahayana who, having given rise to bodhichitta, has vowed to attain enlightenment in order to free all sentient beings from samsara. The term encompasses ordinary beings but is particularly associated with those who have attained the enlightenment of the bodhisattva levels.

BODHISATTVA LEVEL   See ten bhumis.

BRAHMA APERTURE (*tshang bug*; Skt. *brahmarandhra*)   The fontanel at the top of the skull where the hair grows in a circle. Its name originally derives from the Indian belief that the deceased exited through this opening if going to a rebirth in the paradise of Brahma. In the Vajrayana this is the aperture from which the mind exits the body at death in order to gain a good rebirth or even enlightenment.

BUDDHA NATURE (*bde gshegs snying po*; Skt. *tathagatagarbha*) The essence of enlightenment that exists in all sentient beings, which remains unchanged from the state of an ordinary being to buddhahood.

CHAKRA (*'khor lo*) Points on the central channel where subsidiary channels branch off in the manner of spokes from the hub of a wheel. The principal chakras are at the crown of the head, the throat, the heart, and four finger-widths below the navel.

CHANDALI (*gtum mo*) A completion stage practice that develops the union of bliss and emptiness, which is based on a visualization of heat within the body and known for its subsidiary sign of the generation of body heat. It is the first of the Six Yogas of Naropa.

CHANDRAKIRTI (c. 600–50) An Indian master who was a principal exponent of the Madhyamaka school. Chandrakirti is the author of the *Madhyamakavatara (Entering the Middle Way)*, among other texts.

CHANNELS See chakra; nadi, vayu, and bindu.

CHITTAMATRA (*sems tsam*) One of the four schools of Indian Buddhist philosophy studied in Tibet; also known as Yogachara. Founded by Asanga, it holds that appearances are only mind. The name literally means Mind Only.

CHÖD (*gcod*) Literally, cutting. A meditation practice, ideally performed in a frightening location, of offering one's body to the Three Jewels, protectors, all beings, and particularly to demons who wish to devour one's body, in order to accumulate merit, overcome attachment to the self, and realize emptiness.

CLARITY (*gsal ba*) The mind's intrinsic quality of knowing.

COMPLETION STAGE (*rdzogs rim*; Skt. *sampannakrama*) The Vajrayana practice of such methods as the Six Yogas of Naropa, which are practiced on the basis of a creation stage practice. It can also refer to insight meditation practices and at its simplest form to the meditative state following the dissolution of the deity in a creation stage practice.

CREATION STAGE (*bskyed rim*; Skt. *utpattikrama*) Meditation practices involving the generation or creation of a deity and the subsequent visualizations and mantra repetitions.

DAKPO TASHI NAMGYAL (1512–87) The author of *Moonbeams of Mahamudra* and *Clarifying the Natural State.*

DEFILEMENTS See kleshas.

DHARMADHATU (*chos dbyings*) The empty nature of phenomena, although in other contexts it can mean the entire expanse of relative phenomena.

DHARMAKAYA (*chos sku*) See three kayas.

DHARMAKIRTI (seventh century) An Indian master associated with the Chittamatra school who was, after Dignaga, the founder of the Buddhist tradition of logic.

DHARMATA (*chos nyid*) The true nature of phenomena.

DHATUS (*khams*) Elements. The eighteen dhatus consist of the twelve ayatanas (the six sense faculties and six sense objects) together with the six sense consciousnesses.

DIGNAGA (fifth century) The first great master of Indian Buddhist logic and epistemology.

DOHA (*mgur*) A spontaneously composed song expressing one's realization. In India dohas were originally composed of two-line verses.

DZOGCHEN (*rdzogs pa chen po*) Literally, Great Perfection. The highest teachings of the Nyingma and Bön schools.

EIGHT CONSCIOUSNESSES While the Madhyamaka tradition accepts the existence of only six consciousnesses—the five sensory consciousnesses (visual, auditory, olfactory, gustatory, and tactile) and the sixth mental consciousness—the Chittamatra school teaches an additional seventh and eighth consciousnesses—the afflicted (seventh) consciousness and the ground (eighth) consciousness.

FIRST TURNING OF THE WHEEL OF DHARMA This includes the first teaching given by the Buddha. It covers such topics as the Four

Noble Truths, the law of karma, and the emptiness of the self of individuals. It is the basis for the earliest traditions of Buddhism, which within the Mahayana are classed as Hinayana teachings.

FIVE AGGREGATES (*phung po lnga*; Skt. *skandha*) The five physical and mental constituents of beings. They are aggregations of form (*gzugs*), feeling (*tshor ba*), identification (*'du shes*), mental activity (*'du byed*), and consciousness (*rnam shes*).

FIVE BUDDHAS In the highest yoga tantra tradition there is a system of five buddha families: Vairochana (the Buddha family in the center), Akshobhya (the Vajra family in the east), Ratnasambhava (the Ratna, or Jewel, family in the south), Amitabha (the Padma, or Lotus, family in the west), and Amoghasiddhi (the Karma, or Action, family in the north).

FIVE PATHS (*lam lnga*) The five stages of the path to enlightenment within the Hinayana and Mahayana traditions: the path of accumulation, the path of juncture, the path of seeing, the path of meditation, and the path of no more learning, the latter being the final result (that of an arhat in the Hinayana and of buddhahood in the Mahayana).

FIVE POISONS See kleshas.

FIVE WISDOMS (*ye shes lnga*) The five wisdoms of buddhahood: dharmadhatu wisdom (*chos dbyings ye shes*), mirrorlike wisdom (*me long lta bu'i ye shes*), equality wisdom (*mnyam nyid ye shes*), discriminating wisdom (*sor rtogs ye shes*), and accomplishing wisdom (*bya grub ye shes*). They are correlated with the five buddha families and the five poisons, which are transmuted into these wisdoms.

FORM KAYAS See three kayas.

FOUR ACTIVITIES (*phrin las bzhi*) Four kinds of rites, or four types of activities performed by enlightened beings in order to benefit others: peaceful, increasing, controlling, and wrathful.

FOUR IMMEASURABLES (*tshad med bzhi*) Unlimited love, compassion, joy, and equanimity. Also called the *brahmaviharas*, as they are derived from a pre-Buddhist tradition and were said to lead to rebirth in the realm of Brahma.

FOUR YOGAS (*rnal 'byor bzhi*) The four stages presented in the Mahamudra path: one-pointedness (*rtse gcig*), simplicity (*spros bral*), one taste (*ro gcig*), and nonmeditation (*sgom med*).

GAMPOPA (1079–1153) Sonam Rinchen, also known as Dakpo Rinpoche, Gampopa was a physician-turned-monk who became a student of Milarepa and the founder of the first Kagyu monastery, Dalha Gampo, and thus the founder of the monastic tradition of the Kagyu. He was the teacher of Dusum Khyenpa, the first Karmapa.

GENERAL AND SPECIAL PRELIMINARIES The foundation practices of the Vajrayana. The general preliminaries are contemplation of the four thoughts that turn the mind to the Dharma: precious human birth, impermanence, karma, and the defects of samsara. The special preliminaries (*sngon 'gro*) are the four practices of refuge and prostration, Vajrasattva mantra recitation, mandala offering, and guru yoga.

GÖTSANGPA (1189–1258) A student of Tsangpa Gyare, who founded the Drukpa Kagyu lineage, Götsangpa founded the "upper" or "western" branch of the Drukpa Kagyu.

GROUND CONSCIOUSNESS (*kun gzhi'i rnam shes*; Skt. *alayavijñana*) The eighth consciousness, also called the ground consciousness, is the basis for the arising of the other seven consciousnesses and the repository for karmic causes. See also eight consciousnesses.

GURU RINPOCHE A name given to Padmakara, or Padmasambhava, the great master venerated as a second Buddha, who was influential in the introduction of the Dharma to Tibet during the reign of King Trisong Detsen in the eighth century. He is the source of certain *kama* (continually transmitted) and most *terma* (subsequently discovered) practices of the Nyingma tradition.

GURU YOGA A meditation practice of cultivating devotion and receiving the blessings of the lama and the lineage. One of the four special preliminary practices.

HEART SUTRA (*shes rab snying po'i mdo*) The *Essence of Wisdom Sutra,* the shortest of the Perfection of Wisdom sutras, only a few pages long, in contrast with the longest version, *The Hundred Thousand Verse Perfection of Wisdom.* See also Prajñaparamita.

HINAYANA (*theg pa dman pa*) Literally, Lesser Vehicle. The teachings based on the first turning of the wheel of Dharma. The final goal

of the Hinayana path is considered in the Mahayana to be that of
the arhat, though these schools, such as the Theravada, also have
the alternative of making a commitment to become a bodhisattva,
one who aims to achieve buddhahood through a much longer path
of the accumulation of merit.

JAMGÖN KONGTRUL LODRO THAYE (1813–99) A Kagyu master of
the Rimé, or ecumenical, movement. He left an extensive body of
teachings known as the five treasures, which range from the three-
volume *Treasury of Knowledge* to the fifty-four-volume *Treasury of
Termas*.

KAGYU (*bka' brgyud*) One of the four principal traditions of Tibetan
Buddhism, founded by Marpa, which has included many lineages,
such as the Tsalpa, Drukpa, Drigung, Talung, and Karma Kagyu.

KALACHAKRA (*dus kyi 'khor lo*) Literally, wheel of time. A tantra which
is a further development beyond the other highest yoga tantras and
is therefore sometimes classed by itself as the nondual tantra.

KARMAPA The successive heads of the Karma Kagyu lineage. The
Karmapas were the first incarnate lamas recognized in Tibet. The
first Gyalwa Karmapa, Dusum Khyenpa (1110–93), was a student
of Gampopa. The seventeenth Karmapa, Ogyen Trinley Dorje,
was born in 1985.

KLESHAS (*nyon mongs*) The five defilements, afflictions, or poisons: attachment or desire, anger or aggression, ignorance, pride, and
envy.

LAMA SHANG (1123–94) Tsöndru Drakpa, founder of the Tsalpa
Kagyu. He was a student of Dakpo Gomtsul, Gampopa's nephew
and successor at his monastery, Dalha Gampo. Along with Gampopa, Lama Shang was one of the first great Kagyu authors and an
exponent of theocratic rule.

MACHIG LABDRÖN (1031–1129) A disciple of Padampa Sanggye, she
is the source of a widespread lineage of the chöd practice.

MADHYAMAKA (*dbu ma*) The Middle Way. One of the four Indian

Buddhist traditions of philosophy studied in Tibet. It was founded by Nagarjuna, and its later masters include Chandrakirti and Shantideva. Based in particular on the Perfection of Wisdom sutras, it emphasizes the teachings of emptiness and compassion.

MAHAMUDRA (*phyag rgya chen po*)   Literally, Great Seal. Teachings on the practice of directly realizing the mind's true nature. It is taught that everything is "stamped by the seal" of the true nature, so that in the mind there is nothing to be eliminated and nothing to be added. It is particularly based on the songs of the siddha Saraha and the works of subsequent masters such as Tilopa, Naropa, and Maitripa.

MAHASIDDHA (*grub thob*)   The eighty-four mahasiddhas were Indian masters who had accomplished the goal of the Vajrayana while living a diverse variety of lifestyles. They include figures of great importance for the Tibetan Kagyu lineage, such as Saraha, Luyipa, Tilopa, Naropa, and Dombhipa.

MAHAYANA (*theg pa chen po*)   Literally, Great Vehicle, a term introduced by the *Lotus Sutra*. It is composed of the teachings of the Buddha's second and third turnings of the wheel of Dharma.

MAITREYA (*byams pa*)   The fifth Buddha of our eon, said to be residing in the Tushita paradise. Maitreya was appointed regent by Shakyamuni Buddha before he took birth in our world as the fourth Buddha.

MAITREYANATHA   Author of six texts in the Tibetan canon. One is a commentary on a text by Nagarjuna; the other five are popularly known as the Five Teachings of Maitreya. In the Tibetan tradition he is usually identified with Maitreya. It is also argued that he was a fourth-century Indian master (c. 270–350) whose name means "He Who Has Maitreya as His Lord."

MANTRAYANA   See Vajrayana.

MARPA LOTSAWA (c. 1010–95)   Marpa the Translator, a student of the Indian master Naropa and teacher of Milarepa. He was a Tibetan layman who made several journeys to India in order to bring Dharma teachings to Tibet and thereby originated the Karma Kagyu lineage in Tibet.

MENTAL EVENTS (*sems byung*)   Within the Abhidharma tradition there is a classification of fifty-one types of mental events, which are subdivided into five ever-present mental events, five determinative mental states, eleven virtuous mental events, twenty-six negative mental events, and four variable mental events.

MIDDLE WAY SCHOOL   See Madhyamaka.

MILAREPA (1040–1123)   Milarepa was a yogin student of Marpa and the teacher of Gampopa. He spent his life in solitary mountain hermitages and was famous throughout Tibet as a result of the 1488 biography and song collection composed and compiled by Tsangnyön Heruka.

MIND ONLY SCHOOL   See Chittamatra.

NADI   See nadi, vayu, and bindu.

NADI, VAYU, AND BINDU (*rtsa rlung thig le*)   The nadis (*rtsa*) are the subtle channels of the body, through which travel vayu (*rlung*), the subtle airs or winds of the body, one of which is prana (*srog rlung*), the life-force wind. Bindus (*thig le*) are concentrated drops of vital energy that are carried on the winds.

NAGARJUNA (c. second century)   The Indian scholar who is renowned for his texts expounding the logical arguments for emptiness, such as the *Mulaprajña*, which form the basis for the Madhyamaka tradition.

NAROPA (956–1040)   Indian mahasiddha and a pandita at Nalanda University. He was a student of Tilopa and transmitted what became the essential Kagyu instructions to Marpa.

NATURAL PRESENCE (*lhun grub*)   That which does not need to be created. This includes the natural appearance of phenomena and the true nature of mind, thoughts, and appearances in particular.

NIRMANAKAYA (*sprul sku*)   See three kayas.

NIRVANA (*mya ngan las 'das pa*)   The Sanskrit literally means "extinguished"; the Tibetan translation is "transcendence of suffering." Nirvana is liberation from samsara into a state of quiescent peace, though the Mahayana teaches an inseparability of samsara and nirvana, also called "the great nirvana," in which there is a continued activity that benefits beings.

OBSCURATIONS (*sgrib pa*)   Obscurations are of two types: the obscuration caused by the defilements (kleshas) and the obscuration of
knowledge, that is, ignorance of the true nature of phenomena.

PAGMO DRUPA (1110–70)   Dorje Gyaltsen, one of the principal disciples of Gampopa and the founder of the Pagdru Kagyu lineage.
Eight of his students originated lineages, known as the eight junior
or secondary lineages, which include the Drukpa, Drigung, and
Talung.

PARAMITAS (*pha rol tu phyin pa*)   The Sanskrit literally means "perfection"; the Tibetan translation is "crossed over." The six paramitas
are: generosity, discipline, patience, exertion, meditation, and wisdom. There is also a system of ten perfections, adding method,
prayer, power, and knowledge to the initial six.

PEMA KARPO (1527–92)   The fourth Drukchen, head of the Drukpa
Kagyu school, and its greatest scholar. Among many other works,
he is the author of *The Explanation on the Mahamudra Upadesha: The
Treasury of the Victorious Ones*.

PERFECTION OF WISDOM   See Prajñaparamita.

POISONS   See kleshas.

PRAJÑAPARAMITA (*shes rab kyi pha rol tu phyin pa*)   The sixth paramita,
the perfection of wisdom. The Prajñaparamita sutras expound the
doctrine of emptiness and are classed as the second turning of the
wheel of Dharma.

PRAMANA (*tshad ma*)   The teachings of Buddhist epistemology and
logic.

PRELIMINARIES   See general and special preliminaries.

PRINCIPAL MIND (*gtso sems*)   As distinguished from the mental events
that arise in the sixth consciousness. See also mental events.

RANGJUNG DORJE (1284–1339)   The third Karmapa, an important
systematizer and author of the early Karma Kagyu corpus of teachings.

RATNA LINGPA (1403–79)   A renowned *tertön* (treasure revealer) of
the Nyingma lineage.

RATNASAMBHAVA   See five buddhas.

RELATIVE TRUTH   See two truths.

ROOT GURU (*rtsa ba'i bla ma*)   The lama from whom one has received the teachings and instructions that form the core of one's practice.

RUPAKAYA (*gzugs sku*)   See three kayas.

SAMADHI (*ting nge 'dzin*)   Meditative concentration.

SAMBHOGAKAYA (*longs sku*)   See three kayas.

SAMSARA (*'khor ba*)   The cycle of death and rebirth characterized by ignorance and suffering.

SARAHA   One of the Indian mahasiddhas, Saraha was a high-caste Brahmin who is said to have gone to live with a low-caste arrow-maker as his consort. He composed the dohas of the king, the queen, and the people. Saraha is the first human teacher of the Mahamudra lineage, having received it in a vision from Matiratna, a bodhisattva in the entourage of the primordial buddha Vajradhara.

SAUTRANTIKA (*mdo sde pa*)   Followers of Sutra. One of the four schools of Indian Buddhist philosophy studied in Tibet. A branch of the Sarvastivada that classed the Abhidharma as only commentarial in status and emphasized the primacy of the sutras, hence its name.

SECOND TURNING OF THE WHEEL OF DHARMA   The Buddha's Mahayana teachings on compassion and the emptiness of phenomena, such as the Perfection of Wisdom sutras.

SHAKYAMUNI BUDDHA (c. 490–410 B.C.E.)   The historical Buddha. The dates of his lifetime have been subject to successive revisions, the latest findings pointing to a life entirely within the fifth century B.C.E.

SHAMATHA (*zhi gnas*)   Tranquillity meditation.

SHANTARAKSHITA (eighth century)   Indian scholar and first abbot of Samye, the first Tibetan Buddhist monastery.

SHANTIDEVA (c. 685–763)   A principal exponent of the Madhyamaka school and the author of the *Bodhicharyavatara (Entering the Way of Life of the Bodhisattva)*.

SHRAVAKA (*nyan thos*)   Literally, disciple. A Hinayana practitioner who follows the teachings of the Buddha, as opposed to the *pratyekabuddha*s, who attain the Hinayana realization entirely through their own unguided contemplation at a time when the teachings do not exist in the world.

SHUNYATA (*stong pa nyid*) Emptiness; the absence of reality in phenomena.

SIDDHA See mahasiddha.

SIDDHI (*dngos grub*) Spiritual accomplishment. Siddhis are of two types: general and ultimate. General siddhis are supernormal powers such as clairvoyance. Ultimate siddhi is complete enlightenment.

SIX YOGAS OF NAROPA The contents of the list of six has varied considerably. The present-day version has the practices of chandali (inner heat), illusory body, dream, clear light, bardo, and the ejection of consciousness.

SKANDHAS See five aggregates.

SUTRAS (*mdo*) The discourses of Shakyamuni Buddha that comprise the teachings of the Hinayana and Mahayana, in contrast to the tantras, which contain the Vajrayana teachings.

TANTRAS (*rgyud*) The texts of the Vajrayana. In the Kagyu tradition they are classified into four levels: kriya, charya, yoga, and niruttara (or anuttara) yoga tantras.

TEN BHUMIS (*sa*) The ten levels or stages of realization of the enlightened bodhisattva.

THERAVADA A contemporary school of Buddhism that has its origins among the early schools of Buddhism, where it developed as a branch of the Sthavira. It is practiced in Sri Lanka, Burma, Thailand, and southeast Asia. One volume of the Tibetan canon of sutras, *The Miscellania of the Perfection of Wisdom*, is a direct translation into Tibetan of Pali texts of the Theravada. Many other Sarvastivada sutras and Vinaya texts in the Tibetan canon correspond with works in the Pali canon. The Theravada's most famous text, the *Dhammapada*, was not translated into Tibetan until the twentieth century.

THIRD TURNING OF THE WHEEL OF DHARMA The sutras on buddha nature and on all phenomena as manifestations of the mind.

THREE JEWELS (*dkon mchog gsum*; Skt. *triratna*) The Buddha (*sangs rgyas*), the Dharma (*chos*), and the Sangha (*dge 'dun*).

THREE KAYAS (*sku gsum*; Skt. *trikaya*)   Literally, three bodies. The dharmakaya, sambhogakaya, and nirmanakaya, which are aspects of buddhahood. The dharmakaya, or truth body, is a buddha's own realization, experienced only by a buddha. The sambhogakaya, or enjoyment body, is a continuous, divine manifestation perceived only by enlightened beings. The nirmanakaya, or emanation body, is the manifestation in the world, such as the historical Buddha, which can be perceived by ordinary beings. The nirmanakaya and sambhogakaya are known collectively as the rupakaya, or form body, which benefits others; the dharmakaya benefits the buddha alone.

TILOPA (928–1009)   Bengali mahasiddha whose teachings are the origin of the Tibetan Kagyu lineage. Tilopa was the teacher of Naropa.

TÖGAL (*thod rgal*)   Literally, jumping levels. Originally an Abhidharma term. A set of Dzogchen practices that involve spontaneous appearances of lights. The practices entail a retreat in complete darkness and meditation on sunlight.

TWO TRUTHS   The Mahayana teaching on the inseparability of emptiness and appearance. Ultimate, or absolute, truth, is the empty nature of phenomena. Relative truth is the unceasing arising of phenomena.

ULTIMATE TRUTH   See two truths.

VAIBHASHIKA   One of the four Indian Buddhist traditions of philosophy studied in Tibet. A branch of the Sarvastivada, it stressed the importance of the Abhidharma, which it considered to be the actual teaching of the Buddha. The name is derived from their most important text, the *Vibhasha*.

VAIROCHANA   See five buddhas.

VAJRADHARA (*rdo rje 'chang*)   Literally, Vajra Holder. The primordial or dharmakaya buddha, depicted in sambhogakaya form as a blue deity holding a vajra and bell.

VAJRASATTVA (*rdo rje sems dpa'*)   Literally, Vajra Being. A yidam deity that is said to embody all yidam deities. The purification practice of the preliminaries is based on a visualization of Vajrasattva.

VAJRAVARAHI (*rdo rje phag mo*)   Literally, Vajra Sow. A red female yidam deity from the *Chakrasamvara Tantra*. Hers is the most important deity practice in the Karma Kagyu tradition.

VAJRAYANA (*rdo rje'i theg pa*)   Literally, the Way of the Thunderbolt. The Vajrayana teaches skillful means that bring a swift result. Also called Mantrayana because of its use of mantras in the context of deity visualization.

VIPASHYANA (*lhag mthong*)   Meditation that develops insight into the nature of the mind; also, the realization attained through insight meditation.

WANGCHUK DORJE (1555–1603)   The ninth Karmapa, Wangchuk Dorje composed over ten major treatises on philosophy and practice, but the best known are his three instructional works on Mahamudra: *Pointing Out the Dharmakaya, Eliminating the Darkness of Ignorance,* and *An Ocean of the Ultimate Meaning.*

YANGGÖNPA (1213–58)   Principal disciple of Götsangpa who died the same year as his teacher.

YIDAM (*yi dam*)   Literally, "the deity of one's mental commitment."A meditation deity visualized in Vajrayana practice. A yidam embodies particular aspects of enlightened mind.

Index

Abhidharma, 4
Abhidharmakosha, 35, 183n2
Abhidharmasamuccaya, 183n2
Adornment of the Middle Way, The, 115
actions, negative, 49
aggregates, five, 65–66
agitation, 49, 150
    cutting through, 44–45
    eliminating, 42–44
Akshobhya Buddha, 150
alaya, 114
Amitabha Buddha, 149, 150
Amoghasiddhi Buddha, 150
anger, 102–3
anuttara tantra, 174
appearances, 140–41
    as mind, 110–15
    dreamlike, 114
    See also phenomena
arhat, 67
Asanga, 183n2
attachment, 123–24, 130–31, 141–42
Avalokiteshvara, 33
awareness. *See rigpa*
awareness and emptiness. *See rigtong*
ayatanas, 66

bardo, 150–51
bases. *See ayatanas*
"beating the pig's nose," 44–45
Benkar Jampal Zangpo, 51
bhumis, 156
bindus, 150
blessings
    of the guru, 8
    of the lineage, 163–64
bliss, 132
Bodh Gaya, 64
bodhicitta, 124
*Bodhicharyavatara, (Entering the Way of Life
    of the Bodhisattva),* 84
bodhisattva levels, 159–60
Brahma, 64
Brahma aperture, 42

buddha activity, 162
buddhahood, 24, 49, 101, 118, 127–28,
    142, 155–56, 161, 162, 170, 176–79
buddha nature, 69–70
buddha. *See sanggye and individual buddhas*
Buddha Shakyamuni (the Buddha), xvi,
    5, 6, 16, 21, 25, 163–64, 178–79
    Hinayana view of, 64
    Mahayana view of, 64
    qualities, 155–56
    visualization of, 32–33, 34

cause and result, 143–44
    See also karma
chag gya chenpo, 174
Chandrakirti, 68, 84, 85
Chandraprabhakumara, xv
chandali, x, 35
Chittamatra, 108–10, 115, 183n1 (chap. 8)
clarity, 24, 78, 90, 130, 133, 152–53, 154,
    171
compassion, 137, 142–43
conduct, 138, 141
confidence, 48–49
consciousness
    conceptual, 19–20
    eighth (ground) 22–23, 25, 182n1
        (chap. 3)
    seventh (afflicted), 21–22
    sixth (mental), 19–21, 55–58, 77
    visual, 110–12

consciousnesses, 114
    eight, 16–23, 25, 182n2, 182n1
        (chap. 3)
    sensory, 86–87, 114, 118–19
    six, 16–21, 87, 182n2
Creation and Completion, 55
creation stage. *See* deity meditation

Dakpo Tashi Namgyal, 39, 98–99
defilements, 101–3, 124–25, 126
    See also mind poisons; misconcep-
        tions

201

Index

deity meditation, 20–21, 127, 184n2
(chap. 10)
delusion, 92, 152–53, 155
demons, 148–51
deviations (four), 133–36
See also going astray
devotion, 6, 8–9, 51–53, 94
dharmadhatu, 127, 161, 173
dharmakaya, 162, 172–73
Dharmakirti, 85
dharmata, 113
dhatus, 66–67, 161
Dignaga, 85
diligence, 48
directions, the, 125–26
Direct Recognition of the Three Kayas, The, 14
dohas, 180
dullness
cutting through, 44–45
eliminating, 41–42, 149–50
four types of, 150
Dusum Khyenpa, 16
Dzogchen, 115, 167

elements, the, 146
emptiness
and conceptual understanding,
133–34
arising as an enemy, 139
as a remedy, 135
as the path, 135
as natural presence, 117–18
as nature of mind, 95
of mind, 115–17
Nagarjuna on, 84–85, 139–40
sealing with, 134–35
See also phenomena, selflessness
Entering the Middle Way, 85
Entering the Way of Life of the Bodhisattva,
85
errors, eliminating, 59–62
essence, 126
equanimity, 91
experiences, 131–33

Gampo Mountain, xvi
Gampopa, 28, 103, 104, 112–13, 154,
156, 176
as Chandraprabhakumara, xv
lineage, xv–xvi,

meditation experiences of, 131–32
on path Mahamudra, 171
Gateway to Wisdom, The, 68
going astray, 136–38
See also deviations
Gomtsul, 154
Götsangpa, 170
Great Seal, the, 167
Guru Rinpoche, 33
guru yoga, 149–50

happiness, 180
Heart Sutra, xv, 67, 81
Hinayana, 106–8, 124, 128
householder, 3, 180–81
hundred syllable mantra, 51

idleness, 49
illness, 145–48
impermanence, 5–6, 48
Indra, 64
innateness, 176
insight meditation. See vipashyana
insight, partial, 97
interdependence, 68–69

Jamgön Kongtrul, 53
jñana, 152, 161
See also wisdom; yeshe

Kalachakra, 151
karma, 50
See also cause and result
Karma Kagyu tradition, 3
Karmapa, ninth, xvi
Karmapa, sixteenth, 53
Karmapa, third. See Rangjung Dorje
kleshas. See defilements
knowledge, 132

lhag thong, 183n1 (chap. 9)
Lama Mipham, xv, 68
Lama Shang, 126, 154–55, 168
laziness, 49
liberation, 118–19
logic and epistemology. See pramana
Lotus Sutra, 143

Machig Labdrön, 14, 15, 26
Madhyamaka, 115–17, 118
Madhyamakavatara (Entering the Middle
Way), 84

Index

About the Author

The Venerable Khenchen Thrangu Rinpoche is the ninth in a series of Thrangu reincarnations that were based at Thrangu Monastery near Jekundo in the eastern Tibetan region of Gawa. Born in Gawa in 1933, four years later he was recognized as the rebirth of the eighth Thrangu by the sixteenth Karmapa and the eleventh Taisitupa. The young Thrangu Rinpoche studied at the Thrangu monastic college, demonstrating great aptitude in scholarship from an early age.

In 1959, with the Communist suppression of Tibetan monasteries, Thrangu Rinpoche fled to India. That year the sixteenth Karmapa gathered the important lamas who had reached India, including Thrangu Rinpoche, at the monastery of Rumtek in the Himalayan kingdom of Sikkim. The king of Sikkim later donated land near the older Karma Kagyu monastery for a newer and much larger monastery. After obtaining the scholastic degree of Geshe Rabjam, the highest degree awarded in the Gelugpa tradition, in 1968 Thrangu Rinpoche became the khenpo of the new Rumtek Monastery and the tutor for the principal *tulkus* of the Karma Kagyu tradition, including the young twelfth Taisitupa.

Still unable to return to Tibet, in 1979 Thrangu Rinpoche established Thrangu Monastery in Bodhnath, Nepal, where he also founded a school to serve both the young monks of the monastery and lay boys and girls, from a concern that both required a modern education.

Attempting to redress the limited opportunities that women have faced in a traditional context, he established a nunnery in Swayambhu, Nepal, and a school for the young nuns; he provided training for ten nuns to become traditional Tibetan physicians; and he sent some nuns to the university in Sarnath, India. He also founded a three-year retreat for nuns in Manang in northern Nepal.

In 1979 Thrangu Rinpoche also founded a three-year-retreat center in Namo Buddha in the mountains outside the Kathmandu valley, a sacred site associated with a previous life of the Buddha. He subsequently developed this into his principal monastery in Nepal, with its own monastic college as well as a short-term retreat center. A new three-year-retreat center has been founded near Nagarkot, at a site associated with Milarepa. An even more significant project has been the establishment in 1999 of the great monastic college of Vajravidya in Sarnath, the site of the Buddha's first teachings.

While English-speaking Buddhist readers have a wealth of readily available Dharma teachings, ironically Tibetans do not have access to such literature. Therefore Thrangu Rinpoche has established Dharmakara, which publishes texts and edited versions of his teachings in paperback form for a Tibetan readership.

With the lifting of restrictions on religious practice in China in the early 1980s, Thrangu Rinpoche returned to Thrangu Monastery in Gawa for the first of four visits between 1984 and 1996. The monastery, which had been destroyed, has been rebuilt with a new monastic college and retreat center.

In recent decades Thrangu Rinpoche has spent much of each year traveling and teaching at the invitation of centers in the East and the West. Thrangu centers have been established in Malaysia; Taiwan; Hong Kong; Oxford, England; Idyllwild, California; Ellsworth, Maine; Portland, Maine; and Crestone, Colorado, where a retreat center is planned. In 2000, Thrangu Rinpoche was appointed the official tutor of the seventeenth Karmapa, Ogyen Trinley Dorje.